Amazon FBA

Be an Amazon Seller, Launch Private Label Products and Earn Passive Income From Your Online Business

ISBN 978-1-9992202-4-2
Published by Pluto King Publishing

Table of Contents

Chapter 4 – Find a Supplier to Source your Products
100

Chapter 5 – Create your Listing   132

Chapter 6 – Product Launch   154

Chapter 7 – The Aftermath   282

Chapter 8 – Business Structures for your FBA Business   298

Conclusion   306

Bonus Chapter – Beginner's Guide to Merch By Amazon   307

Introduction

If you're bored of your nine-to-five job and looking for simple ways to make a great living from home, this book is especially designed for you, as well as for others who are looking for an online platform to earn and grow an income fast, and/or who want to take ownership of the future and turn a sustainable profit. I have put together a comprehensive guide for selling things on Amazon.

Not only does Amazon's Fulfillment By Amazon (FBA) service help you generate great profits with minimal effort, it also allows you to start your business with almost no start-up costs. You don't need a warehouse, which means no overhead costs. You can become an effective salesperson on this platform and build massive revenue, which continues even when you're not actively involved in the business. I know many people who have started their business on FBA with minimal initial costs and created a six-figure income on the platform. I assure you that you can make this happen; you can make your home-based business a rewarding venture.

Disclaimer

The information in this book is intended for general information purposes only. This book does not provide any legal or tax advice. The author and publisher disclaim any liability in connection with the use of this information. Ask a tax professional or other financial expert for additional assistance if necessary or to see what might apply for someone in your specific situation. The writers, producers and sellers of this guide cannot be held responsible for any problems that might come about during the investment process.

Chapter 1 – What Is FBA and Why Should You Use It?

Amazon FBA

FBA—Fulfillment By Amazon—is a service provided by Amazon that allows you to collect products you want to sell, list them in your seller account and ship those items to Amazon's Fulfillment Center. After that, sales will automatically take place through Amazon.

How to Use FBA

The item you sell can either be from your personal belongings or a private label—a product manufactured by a third party and sold under a brand name. If you are the brand owner, you can buy a product from a third-party manufacturer and brand it under your name. As part of that, you need to specify key details about the product such as what it encompasses, how it should be packaged, how it should look, the design of the label, what features should be listed on the packaging and so on.

Selling on Amazon FBA is simple.

1. Select and send your items to Amazon.

Select the new or used item you want to sell. If it is a private label product, contact the manufacturer to create your product line. Launch your listing on the website so that Amazon can fulfill your products through its fulfillment service. Attach the PDF labels provided by Amazon, or use the label service offered by

FBA. Send the product to Amazon's Fulfillment Center either using their shipping service or your own carrier.

2. Allow Amazon to store your product in its warehouse.

Once Amazon receives your product, it scans it and records pertinent information, such as unit dimensions for storage. You can monitor your product using Amazon's integrated tracking system.

3. Wait for customers to see your products and place an order.

Amazon FBA ranks your listings by price, with no shipping fees included, as the products are eligible for free shipping (certain orders, such as multi-channel fulfillment orders, are excluded). All Prime members can upgrade the options for shipment for FBA listings.

4. Your products are picked and packed by Amazon.

Amazon FBA picks your products from its warehouse and packs them for delivery. The products are located using an advanced web-to-warehouse system, which is a high-end, high-speed sorting and selecting system.

5. The products are shipped to the customers.

Amazon ships the products from its fulfillment centers to the customers. Customers can track their products on the website and customer service is available to them as needed.

What Benefits Does It Offer?

Amazon's large customer base provides an outstanding marketplace for people who want to effortlessly market products or services online to a large group of people. The majority of Amazon customers prefer to purchase products that can be shipped to them via FBA. Amazon, in fact, claims that most customers buy items from a third-party vendor only if the product or service they are providing is Amazon trusted, meaning Fulfilled by Amazon. FBA allows you to target two specific groups of people who might otherwise dismiss your listings due to shipping costs. Sellers who effectively utilize FBA cater to these two key markets:

- **Customers eligible for Super Saver Shipping** – All online buyers who buy products worth at least $25 are eligible for free Super Saver Shipping. These are shoppers who will typically not pay extra for shipping, even if a non-FBA seller offers a product at a lower price. However, such customers don't mind spending an extra dollar or two in order to earn Super Shipping Service.

- **Customers who subscribe to Prime Membership** – Prime Membership guarantees free two-day delivery on all products shipped directly from Amazon's warehouse. By paying the annual Prime membership fee, these customers are making a direct investment in FBA. As a result, they receive their items sooner than if they had purchased them from a potentially lower-priced third-party vendor. For instance, my sister pays a little extra to use FBA to purchase Swiss Miss Hot Marshmallow Cocoa, although she could buy it cheaper from a non-FBA seller. She considers this additional cost a small price to pay to satisfy her taste buds quickly, rather than having to wait days or weeks.

All Prime members are awarded free shipping service for one year until they renew their membership.

Your job as a seller will be simpler and effortless

FBA makes the process of selling items easy. Simply gather your merchandise, enter the details of your items online and email the details to the fulfillment center. Amazon will then help you find buyers, list your items on a dashboard, safely store your items in its warehouses and ship the products to your customers. Furthermore, Amazon will handle customer service. While Amazon is taking care of all the marketing/shipping details, you can then focus your time on your business strategy.

Generate HUGE Profits

In today's highly competitive market, it's not easy to attract business. With millions of people trying to sell their products online and offline, you need to have an edge in the market. Amazon FBA offers you that edge, providing a platform that gives shoppers concrete incentives for choosing FBA items over non-FBA ones. These shoppers have the potential to become loyal customers who don't mind paying a little extra in order to quickly receive quality products or quality services.

Less Competition in a Highly Competitive Marketplace

When you're trying to set a price for your product on Amazon, you don't have to compete with other non-FBA players selling similar items. Your customers will be aware of the quality of service you are offering through Amazon FBA. Price your merchandise fairly and you'll stay competitive—without compromising the profit margins.

Less Overhead Costs

Compare the difference in costs when it comes to shipping your products directly to customers versus using FBA. Do the analysis and you'll discover that shipping your items directly to shoppers requires more packaging material than is required when you use FBA. This may seem like a small expense, but ship enough merchandise and such an expense (or saving) adds up fast.

You Become More Visible in the Marketplace

When a shopper searches the site for a product, the website brings up search results in ascending order of price, with the least expensive at the top of the list. Amazon.com shows its customers the total price, including base price and cost of shipping. Since FBA provides free shipping, the base price that is listed will not factor in shipping costs. Therefore, your items will always appear higher in the search results, improving the visibility of your listed items.

Seamless Customer Experience for Your Clients

Unless you have a dedicated customer service staff, you can't attend to your customers' needs 24/7, much as you might want to. Customer service is another one of the extremely important business details that requires an extensive investment of time. Amazon FBA can provide that 24-hour service, giving you peace of mind as you attend to other important aspects of your business.

Continue Doing Business Even When Not Physically Present

Perhaps you've encountered a situation where you had to temporarily close your Amazon shop and/or had to deactivate product listings because you would not be immediately available to pack and ship your merchandise. You want customers to get their purchases immediately, and any kind of delay is unacceptable. FBA gives you peace of mind. As you take care of other important matters, rest assured that your packages will be sold and shipped in a timely fashion.

Amazon Rules and Features

UPC Requirements

Amazon requires that specific products have barcodes:

- products that are consumable and topical
- items that come with an expiry date and
- those that are not tracked using a manufacturer's barcode.

There are two types of barcodes that can be used to identify products on FBA:

- Manufacturer barcode (UPC, GCID, etc.)
- Amazon barcode (ASIN, FNSKU, etc.)

FBA uses the UPC (Universal Product Code) to identify, track and monitor products throughout the entire fulfillment process.

If you decide to use a manufacturer's barcode for your listings, Amazon can ship items which are closest to a customer's address even if the item is not sent to the fulfillment center. In such cases, you (as the seller) are credited with the sale, and the item is sent from your inventory to the seller.

To safeguard its customers from buying fake products, Amazon reserves the right to remove any listing which has an invalid UPC; they can even suspend your selling privileges. Identification numbers (called GTINs) and licensing by GS1 (a governing body for barcodes) are needed for products and services to uniquely identify brand owners. Amazon prevents its customers from buying fake products on its platform by insisting on these requirements. Amazon also tries to minimize duplicate listings to avoid confusing its customers. It ensures product reviews are genuine. New listings on Amazon must match their designated brands' UPCs as the platform checks for brand, title and manufacturer fields to be accurate.

Important Info

1) GTINs should be purchased only from GS1. If you're a brand owner, you will need a company prefix. The first three numbers identify the country of origin and the remaining numbers indicate the type of product, color, size and so on. This information is then converted into barcodes so that they can be read by machines/apps. In order to know what type of UPC to use, check the barcode classification details provided by GS1.

2) If you haven't purchased the GTINs from GS1, you can use the official online tool to find out if the code is valid. If it is not, you need to take action on it as you are a brand owner. If you are not the brand owner, you can sell your items on the platform as an unauthorized reseller, ensuring you use the original UPC. Be very careful while doing this as these codes might not be genuine. Therefore, it is your responsibility to cross-check to see that the codes are valid before you list the items.

Amazon FNSKU Requirements

Amazon's Fulfillment Network Stock Keeping Unit (FNSKU) is how Amazon recognizes an item and tracks its progress toward the fulfillment center. Once you've created your listing on Amazon, an FNSKU is assigned to your item, printed based on product levels. Each item is then assigned a unique number. Amazon tries to match this unique identifier with the ASIN. If the ASIN matches, it implies that the product is "stickerless commingled inventory," thereby determining whether your inventory will be stored with products from other sellers.

While the UPC helps Amazon track different products, the FNSKU helps track inventory for various sellers in the fulfillment centers. If a product is being sold on Amazon by four different sellers, each seller will have their own FNSKU so that Amazon can keep track of each seller's inventory. Therefore, whenever an item is listed on Amazon for sale, there is a unique UPC generated, and an FNSKU, which is unique to the seller(s) of that product.

FBA Product Restrictions

Before listing your products for FBA, it's important to know what can and can't be sold through the fulfillment process.

Open Product Categories – Most popular items, including toys, books, groceries, kitchenware, etc. can be sold

Gated Product Categories – Amazon 'gates' (requires authorization to sell) certain products in order to protect both sellers and buyers. Gated products include fine art, sports items, handbags, clothes, shoes, watches, sunglasses, appliances, etc. Consider that sellers might have bought certain items from other sellers. The quality could, thus, potentially not be up to Amazon's high standards. Therefore, if your merchandise falls into one of the gated categories, you'll need to prove that your product adheres to Amazon's requirements. For instance, if you're selling entertainment equipment, part of the gated requirement will be a certification by a third-party vendor.

Restricted Product Categories – Amazon guarantees that all products sold on its platform are legal, safe and comply with federal and state laws and regulations. Before you list a product on Amazon, carefully review the different product categories, then consult with legal authorities if you have questions about the policies set forth by Amazon concerning your item. Amazon is constantly working with vendors, third-party experts and sellers to improve ways to prevent the sale of illegal and unsafe products.

Inventory Requirements

FBA Listing Requirements – Follow the guidelines defined by FBA to create titles for your product. The titles must be consistent, have the right information for the ASIN, and match product labels.

Product Title Specifics:

1) Length: There's a max of 50 characters for most (though not all) categories.
2) Capitalization: The first letter of the title should be capitalized; articles and conjunctions should not. Do not use all caps.
3) Symbols and numbers: Always spell out measurements; don't use symbols such as '$.'
4) Product information: Always include color and size in the ASINs. Never include price details, promotional messages, manufacturer or brand details in the title, unless it's a private label.

Shipment Packaging Requirements – It's important to package the product correctly to ensure it reaches Amazon safely and is optimized for the fulfillment centers.

1) Use a sturdy box.
2) Wrap each item separately, using adequate packing material such as shipping tape, bubble wrap, inflatable air pillows and polyethylene foam sheeting. Don't use paper overwrap or twine.
3) Remove all traces of previous labels and/or scannable barcodes, if you are re-using boxes or are using a retail box.
4) One current delivery address should be used.
5) Do not bundle multiple boxes together.
6) Do not use pallet-size boxes and point-of-sale containers.

Inventory Storage Requirements – To effectively manage the space available in the fulfillment centers, Amazon defines storage limits for FBA sellers as the maximum amount of inventory that a seller can store in the FBA fulfillment center. This is automatically calculated every month, with the limit adjusted as per a seller's changing inventory. Inventory storage limits are applicable to all new sellers who have slow-moving inventory. Sometimes storage limits are created even for certain ASINs.

Once a shipment is received at the fulfillment center, it takes about 24 hours for the system to update inventory. Based on how close the inventory is to the defined limit, these indicators are used:

- Green – indicates inventory level is less than 75 percent of the defined limit.
- Yellow – indicates inventory level is between 75 percent and 95 percent of the defined limit.
- Red – indicates inventory level is more than 90 percent of the defined limit.

If you exceed the given limit for your inventory, Amazon will notify you by email, and you will not be able to create new shipments until you clear your space. If the limit has been reached for a specific ASIN, you will not be able to add any of those ASINs to your inventory, but other ASINs will be allowed. In order to reduce the inventory, you can sell some of the inventory or officially request some of it be returned or disposed of.

For FBA Products to be Sold as 'New' on Amazon – For an item to be sold as New on Amazon, it must arrive at the fulfillment center brand new, in perfect condition. If there are any scratches, marks, dents, or wear and tear found on the packaging or item, it will be re-labeled as Used. In order to ensure that customers receive good quality products from sellers, Amazon reserves the right to reject shipments that have not been packaged correctly.

FBA Inventory Placement Requirements

When any shipping plan is created, your shipment might be divided into multiple parts. To better distribute your products, Amazon routes shipments through a center (that receives the inventory) to other fulfillment centers in their network. These products are then put up for sale as soon as they are received at the different fulfillment centers. If the products are being reshipped to another center in the network, they might be made available to customers at a future shipping date.

Generally, most standard-sized items are directed to a single center. However, products belonging to categories such as jewelry, apparel, shoes, hazardous materials, media, etc. might be directed to a different fulfillment center. The division of shipments is also done based on product categories.

Case-packed Products – When individual sellable items are packaged together to form one unit, Amazon respects the packaging and doesn't break the case into separate items. However, these cases must adhere to the following rules:

1) All items in the cased box must have a matching SKU and must have been previously packaged together by the manufacturer.
2) All boxes with the same product must have equal quantities of that product in each box.
3) The maximum case limit for one package is 150 units.
4) Sometimes manufacturers might pack multiple case-packs into a bigger outer box, known as a master carton. These master cartons do not qualify as case-packs and are split at the case-pack level.

Selling on FBA

What to Sell on Amazon

As a beginner, it's always good to learn the secrets of a platform and gain an understanding of what it can offer you before buying costly stock and tools. Starting small and discovering a business from the ground up allows you to get acquainted with every step of the process of selling on Amazon, teaching you what the marketplace is all about. This will help you manage your downtime and recognize your shortcomings. You need to know the marketplace well in order to see if there is anything about Amazon that doesn't work for you and whether there are any issues that should be addressed at an early stage. This approach helps you understand the ins and outs of selling through Amazon FBA. Eventually, you will see that that are many markets that can generate income for you, with the help of FBA.

As a new seller, consider selling unwanted media items (such as CDs, video games) from your house for your first Amazon sale. This is the best way to find out the nuances of doing business on Amazon without having to deal with any serious implications/dangerous purchasing decisions. You need to discover ways of generating profit margins on the Amazon platform by selling items that can earn a 100 percent. For example, if you have a book that you have already read, you have already gotten your money's worth. Consider selling it on Amazon, as any money made from it is actually 100 percent profit.

Besides looking at what's lying around your house, you can also ask your relatives, family members, friends or neighbors if they want to contribute items to help you do business with Amazon. Consider how the world of technology is altering the way people shop and save their media. The world is going digital, and this fact can be used to your benefit. Consider what is compatible with today's e-world, and assess whether any items you have will add value to the type of media people collect today. Don't be deterred because something seems "old fashioned." There's a market for most things including magazines, books, CDs, etc. Scour your house, and don't forget the attic and garage.

The bottom line is to start discovering items to sell— even if it's just a "useless" product which has been lying unused in your basement for months. To know the real worth of your items, study Amazon's marketplace. As you discover the real value of your items on the platform, you will be able to price your items appropriately and will also be able to decide on what can be sold and what needs to be discarded.

Steps to Selling on Amazon

1. Choose Your Niche

Any new venture must start with careful and thorough research, which might be time-consuming. Trust me; it is worth every second you spend. Once you choose your niche, you will be able to come up with ideas easily.

Think about your hobbies and interests. If you are passionate about fashion, consider creating your own fashion line. If you like artwork, you can have your own line of décor items. You will enjoy your new venture more if it is something you are passionate about.

However, make sure you formulate your ideas in a way that they generate good revenue for you. This is important because, at the end of the day, you need to see results in the form of profit margin and growth.

Another place to look for your niche could be your family, relatives, friends, co-workers, or neighbors. Ask them what is it that they want to see in the marketplace—a specific product, a service, a solution, or something else. When you're building a business, you're trying to cater to what people want, what they're looking for, what is it that would help them, etc. Don't forget to also consider what you would like to see and buy

Once you have some ideas, brainstorm and create a list of ideas and products. Now, ask more people, do research online, read forums, reach out to people and get all the required information on those niches. Then, based on the data gathered and your personal interests, narrow down the list to ideas you think are feasible. See if others are also looking for something similar—is there a good-sized market looking for the same product/service? Research and come up with ideas and possible solutions to meet the requirements of your target audience.

Amazon has many product categories (and sub-categories) that can give you ideas. If a category or a sub-category has fewer products associated with it, it doesn't mean it's not popular or liked by shoppers. Look at the reviews people have posted on these products. You can't just go by the number, as quality also makes a huge difference. Another great feature of this platform is that you can look for the best sellers for each category. This can also help you decide on a product or niche you might be interested in.

There are also free and paid tools available in the market that can help you with your product research. What you should be looking for is a product that is selling well or is in demand and has low competition. I will discuss some of the tools in the next chapter.

2. Source a Supplier

You now know what you want to sell. If the product is something from around your house, this step can be skipped as you yourself are a supplier. But if the product doesn't belong to that lonely corner of your house, you need to find a supplier to source you the product as private label. These are manufacturers who make the product and sell it at a wholesale price. Sellers can then brand the product with their own label. Start looking for manufacturers who can supply you with the products you are interested in selling online.

There are a few options available online, such as aliexpress.com, alibaba.com, etc. that will help you source your product. The search results on these websites also provide supplier details. Look for suppliers who are prequalified/trusted by the website.

While looking for source suppliers:

- Research and know your products inside and out. Read product reviews on various websites so you know the features of the product. This will come in handy when discussing the product with the suppliers.

- It's always good to build a base before negotiating prices and terms with suppliers. Strike up a conversation and build a good rapport with them.
- Negotiate till they offer you something lucrative, but be reasonable and fair in your expectations.

3. Set Up an Account

You are now almost ready to sell, but first you need a seller's account on Amazon.

If you're just a beginner, opt for an Individual account. That said, if you're going to sell more than 40 items in a month, you need to have a Professional account. This isn't a site rule, but it makes financial sense for the following reason: Amazon charges $1 per item for an Individual account and $40 per month for a Professional account. So, if you're going to sell more than 40 items in a month, you might as well get a Professional account.

Once you're clear on what type of account you need, create it using your chosen email address. You'll then need to provide further seller information, will have to verify your identity, and finally, will need to provide a charging method. After that, you'll be ready to start selling!

4. Launch Your Product

Okay, so now you have the product, the supplier and a seller's account. Your product is on its way to the

Amazon warehouse. Now, you'll need to optimize how you sell your product, ensuring you use keywords that help you attract your customers. Amazon allows one to four keywords based on your product's category. Adding target-related keywords allows you to be more specific with your product listings. For instance, if you are selling school bags, you can include the target keyword "students."

Use enticing images, catchy headlines and a solid description. It's important to do whatever it takes to get your listing on the first page for searched keywords. Some fundamental ideas and basic rules of using SEO apply to product listings. Always bear in mind that the title of your product listing is the first thing that you can use to catch the attention of your audience. This can be done by using strong, catchy keywords to inform and attract the target audience. It should make sense and convey the right message.

- Amazon recommends product brand names go first for every category of product as they draw attention.
- Amazon recommends using keywords in the title that are normally searched by the customers. An important point to note here is that Amazon doesn't recognize the comma. If you want to separate keywords, just use a space.
- When color is important for a product sale, it should be mentioned toward the end of the title, after the brand name and the required SEO keywords. For instance, if you're planning to sell mobile phones, add the color at the end.

- The length of the product title must never exceed 200 characters in all categories. Since certain categories might specify different maximums for the length of the title, it is always good to know the allowed maximum length for your product category that can be found in style guide.
- Bullets are your best friends. Adding bullet points in your product description will help you draw attention and better inform your target audience. This will give you an opportunity to highlight what's unique about your product and why someone should buy it. When you start adding bullet points to your product listings, Amazon helps you by telling you what it expects you to mention. Amazon has guidelines for creating bullet points:
  - A maximum of 500 characters are allowed, but 30-70 are better
  - Trademark and copyrights infringement are not to be included in Amazon Product Listings
  - Pricing and promotional information must never be included (i.e. "Sale")
  - Listings that describe a set of items should include everything in the set
  - Semicolons should be used to separate phrases in a bullet point
  - Each bullet point should start with a capital letter
  - Don't use end punctuation; sentence fragments are fine
  - Do not use clichéd phrases, such as "best quality product ever."

- "Pictures speak louder than words" holds true for your product listings. Amazon lets you upload up to seven images of your product. These images have to be specific dimensions in order to enable the zooming feature that Amazon offers so that buyers can hover a mouse over the pictures to see key features and details. Take advantage of this feature by providing pictures that are at least 1000 x 1000 pixels.

- Persuade and inform your potential customers using impactful product descriptions. These descriptions do not have to be unique; they can even be copied from another site. Amazon doesn't require you to write them, unlike Google, which wants all the descriptions to be unique. Amazon just needs correct grammar, coherent content and relevant details. In addition to the standard five bullet points, Amazon lets you add content of up to 2000 characters. This is another place for you to use to target keywords. These can even be the keywords that you used in the product description title on Amazon.

- Add specifications for your product to differentiate it from others in the market. This is another effective way to give you an edge over other similar competitive items in the marketplace. Give the platform what it wants in terms of SEO specifications, such as dimensions, etc. Sellers often miss this information, but they don't know that this does make a difference in the numbers. It is considered an important factor which determines the ranking of the product. Some buyers want to see this kind of information and Amazon will see you as a serious seller if you use it. Diligent sellers are rewarded with Amazon's rating.

- Price is key to drawing customers, of course. Being a seller, you can modify and play around with the product's price on Amazon dashboard to make it competitive. You can even create deals on the products by entering the normal selling price and then slashing it by a defined percentage. You must have seen such listings which say list price and then have a sale price in bright red below the list price. Sometimes the difference in the amount is marked as a discount in terms of percentage, and sometimes it is a fixed amount.

Get Sales and Reviews: When you start for the first time, you should aim for two things—good reviews and sufficient sales. If you get these two things, it's going to give you the momentum you need to get ranked on popular platforms and eventually generate revenue.

Your aim should be to make sure your items are listed in the search results given by Amazon, and if possible, among the top results. When anyone enters the name of your product and it appears in the top listing, half the battle is won because the general tendency of shoppers is to just browse through the first few pages. One way to improve your ranking is sales. The more you sell, the better your position on the list.

In today's competitive world, there will be many other players who might be selling the same product as you. This is where reviews come into the picture. Before purchasing anything, shoppers look at reviews. If your product has mostly positive feedback, you're far more likely to sell. An effective way to improve your reviews is by signing up for tools such as Salesbacker that help you to grow your product reviews.

Run Campaigns: Run promotional campaigns, submit press releases and ask people to promote your business to their extended network. Post frequently on all social media platforms and do whatever it takes to spread the word. Look for influential bloggers with large followings and work with them to promote your business. The more people know about you, the better.

Amazon FBA Fee Structure

By now you know that working with Amazon can be really advantageous. But Amazon itself is a business, of course, and has to charge a price for the various services it offers. Here are things that you must keep in mind while working out the seller's cost of your merchandise. There might be some variation in fees due to:

- price/weight/size of each product.
- duration the product is stored.
- type of product.
- change in Amazon fee structure.
- addition/removal of fee types by Amazon.

While estimating the profit margin on each product you sell on the platform, also take into account all the possible charges levied by Amazon for selling a product using their FBA service:

Seller Account Fees – These are the basic fees for selling your products on Amazon. You can choose from the two pricing plans—Individual and Pro Merchant. When you're just starting a business using FBA, you should choose the Individual plan (this means paying Amazon a fixed rate at the close of sale for each item). With an Individual account:

- You're allowed to sell up to 40 items per month.
- An inventory management facility is NOT available.
- You're allowed to sell products only within certain categories.

Once you get the hang of it, you can upgrade your account to a Pro Merchant account. This means paying a fixed price to Amazon for selling each product using their service, which is slightly higher than what you would pay for the Individual plan. With a Pro account:

- You can have unlimited product listings.
- You can sell more than 40 items per month.
- You're connected to the order management and e-commerce platforms.
- You have an option for inventory management.

Sale-related Fees – As part of this, you pay an amount to Amazon when you actually sell products on their website. The amount that you pay varies based on what you're selling and the product's price. These fees are divided into three types:

- **Referral Fees** – Amazon applies a referral fee (commission) on the sale of books and all other media items. This is normally a small percentage of the selling price of your item on Amazon, for example, 15 percent of the selling price of an item. There are two attributes that define the referral fees—the product category and your selling price.

- **Minimum Referral Fees** – There is a minimum referral fee that Amazon assigns to some of its product categories. This is normally around $1-$2, depending on the category to which your product belongs. If there is a minimum referral fee applicable to your listed item, you will have to pay the greater of the two fees—referral or minimum referral, not both. You can see which product categories have minimum referral fees on the website.
- **Variable Closing Fees** – This is a fixed amount that is based on the type of item that is being sold on Amazon. The variable closing differs for different types of items. It's a flat fee of $1.80 that is added on top of the referral fee of the product that belongs to the defined types, including media items.

Pick and Pack Fees – These are the fees that Amazon charges for FBA listings and is normally calculated according to the time a person spends on finding your item in their warehouse and packaging it for shipping. This is the price associated only with FBA listed items, and both Individual and Pro Sellers have to pay this amount if they use FBA to stock, pick, pack and ship their items.

FBA fees are based on the size and weight of the items, as well as the time of the year. The FBA fee structure is quite streamlined, and Amazon considers picking, packing and shipping under one heading and inventory storage under another heading. It includes the fees for boxes and containers, and it even covers returns from buyers. This component of the fees also depends on the size of the product you're going to store and ship. FBA products are divided into two types based on the size of packaging:

- Standard-sized products—these are standard-sized items that are fully packaged and weigh less than 20 pounds. The maximum size allowed for this category is 18" x 14" x 8".
- Oversized products—these are items with sizes that exceed 18" x 14" x 8" and/or weigh more than 20 pounds.

Weight Handling Fees – This fee depends on the weight of the item being sold on Amazon FBA. If the item weighs more, the fees will be more, and vice versa. You might know how much your item weighs, but to calculate this fee component, Amazon will also weigh it.

Storage Fees – Amazon charges storage fees to sellers who use their FBA service at a rate for each cubic foot of storage space the item occupies in the fulfillment center. This fee varies with the time of the year the item is stored. For example—the fee increases during the months of October, November and December.

The Amazon storage fee is something every seller should be aware of because you might end up paying a huge amount which can eat up your profit margin; it can even cause you to lose money on your products. Therefore, it is recommended that you access the storage fees on a regular basis and adjust your strategy to maximize your profit margin. As Amazon grows, it needs to stay ahead of the game by keeping space open in the fulfillment centers in order to satisfy customers. As the business builds, the space fills, and space is in high demand.

There are therefore two types of fees related to storage that you should be familiar with:

- **Monthly Inventory Storage fees** – Since space is at a premium in the fulfillment centers, the greater the inventory you store in the warehouse, the higher the fees will be. The storage fees depend on the daily average volume of storage space the inventory occupies in the fulfillment centers. Amazon does the calculation to determine how much you owe for Monthly Inventory Storage fees, and specifies it in Seller Central (which is the dashboard available to Amazon sellers). Amazon reserves the right to do its own measurements and weigh any packaged units. If there are any conflicts between what they measure and information you provided, they have the right to govern and settle the dispute.

  Again, there are two headings under which the rates are categorized—the standard size of the unit and oversize. Although standard-sized packages may take less space, sometimes their storage can be complicated as compared to the oversized packages because the fulfillment centers have drawers and bins to store products. While the fees to store oversized packaged products are higher, Amazon can require extra fees to store standard-sized packages depending on how complex the storage is.

- **Long-term Storage Fees** – On February 15 and August 15 every year, Amazon conducts a cleanup activity for its inventory to assess Long-Term Storage fees. Generally, Amazon charges a fixed amount per cubic foot of space occupied by an item that has been stored there for six to twelve months. For any products in the warehouse for longer than 12 months, the amount is slightly more. Long-term storage fees help Amazon to provide quality service to all their sellers and their customers.

There are various ways to determine whether your units will be subjected to Long-Term Storage fees. There are different tools within Seller Central that you can use to determine this so that you can plan a strategy to avoid these fees.

One such tool is the FBA Inventory Age Box that is available within the Inventory Dashboard. Here's how to use it:

o Hover your mouse over the Inventory tab within Seller Central and click on Manage Inventory from the drop-down list.
o Click on Inventory Dashboard and scroll down till you see the FBA Inventory Age Box.
o Click View Details.
o This should help you find the estimated Long-Term Storage fees and the inventory age for your products.

Another option to get a sense of whether you will accrue a long-term fee is to utilize the Inventory Health report available in Seller Central as it helps to understand which units and fees fall into each of the two categories—six to twelve months and 12+ months. To access this report:

o Hover your mouse over Reports within Seller Central and then click on Fulfillment from the drop-down menu.
o Select the Show More option from the inventory tab on the screen. Select Inventory Health.
o There are various fields within this report that indicate the number of units subjected to Long-Term Storage fees within the two categories and the estimated Long-Term Storage fees for each.

To avoid storage fees:

o Use strategies to stock your inventory. Start with small quantities. This will give you a sense of how soon you will sell your products. You should always store more inventory than you think will sell in six months. Planning for a six-month period ensures that you don't run out of stock. Avoid sending large quantities just before the inventory cleanup date.

o You can store inventory in a different location than the Amazon warehouse such as your workplace, your house, your garage, etc. When you see the product moving, you can replenish it quickly so that you don't run out of stock. This way you will have more flexibility in terms of managing your inventory versus sending all the products to the Amazon warehouse for storage at one time.

o Offer discounts on inventory that has been sitting in the storehouse. When you see you are getting close to the cleanup dates, run a discount offer or a price-cut promotion so that this inventory can move out quickly. Inside of Seller Central, Amazon allows sellers to use different campaigns. Headline Search campaigns and Sponsored Product campaigns are the two main ways to enhance your sales.

o If all the above methods do not seem to be helping you and if the inventory cleanup date is approaching, consider fully or partly clearing the inventory that is at risk. You can create a removal order to get this done. But do it only if it makes sense. The best way to determine whether it would help you or not is to do some math. Take the Long-Term Storage fees within the Inventory Health report and add these fees into the profit margin calculator. If you see this fee component will cause you to lose your profit, using one of these strategies is a smart move.

You might observe a minor plus or minus in these components while selling your merchandise. For instance, an additional fee could be charged on a book that lies in the Amazon warehouse for five months before getting sold. But the important thing to note here is that you will be taking advantage of Amazon's multifold benefits for just a small additional amount.

You can make significant profits by selling your items with Amazon FBA. Always remember that not every product you list on Amazon will rack up more in fees than your profit. With experience and time, you can sell only the items that generate larger profits. When you're new and are getting acquainted with this market, the focus should be on selling. Look at it this way—your item might be just lying in the shelves of a store for months, but when you put it on Amazon, you might earn a small $1 profit each time a copy is sold on Amazon. Amazon has loyal customers, so the probability of your item getting sold there is higher than in a common store.

The more you practice listing your merchandise on Amazon, the more confidence you will gain and eventually it will take you just a few minutes to do the listings. With some more guidance and research, you will see how easy it is to transform a new account into a money-making business.

How to Estimate the FBA Fees

Now that you know about the different fee schedules, let's look at what you need to know to estimate Amazon fees.

- ✓ The shipping dimensions—length, width and weight—for each product.
- ✓ The price you're going to sell the product on Amazon.
- ✓ How to use Amazon Fee calculator.

Once you have all these things, you can follow the step-by-step process outlined below:

1. **Find** products similar to what you're trying to sell on Amazon.

Log on to Amazon and look for items similar to your product so that you can come up with the most accurate estimate of the Amazon FBA fees. The main attributes that you should be looking for are product dimensions, shipping weight and the category of the product. Make sure the match you find belongs to the same product category as that of your product.

2. **Fetch** the ASIN details for the shortlisted similar product.

Once you find a match for your product, browse through the page that matches your product closely and then look for the Product Details section. Note the ASIN number as this needs to be used in the following step.

3. **Use the Amazon Fee Calculator** to evaluate the FBA fees.

Go to the Amazon FBA Fee Calculator and enter this number on the page that opens. Search for the entered number, and you might see a screen pop up. If it does, choose the item that you were looking for. Once that's done, you will see that the calculator is ready to give you the estimated fees.

4. **Fee Calculation** based on the Selling Price of the product.

Enter your product's price in the right Amazon Fulfillment column and then press the Calculate button.

5. **Time** to evaluate the data

You now have a lot of data to analyze, but the most important data is located on the right side of the page, highlighted in yellow. This is where you will see the fees Amazon has estimated for your product. You have all the details of what they are going to charge. It might be overwhelming to look at the details but just pay attention to the last three rows to find the gist—the Fulfillment Cost Subtotal, the Cost Subtotal and the Margin Impact. The Cost Subtotal is the fee Amazon will charge, and the Margin Impact is the amount of profit you will make after deducting the fees.

When to Use the FBA Calculator?

One of the best uses of the FBA calculator is while looking for new products. When you're researching what product to sell, using the FBA calculator can give you a sense of profit that you can make when it sells. Another great use of this calculator is to evaluate the impact on your profit margin if you lower or raise the product cost or selling price of the product. This will give you an understanding of what kind of cost range you should use or what should be the minimum price for an item while remaining profitable. The calculator can also be used when you're trying to switch your business model from merchant-fulfilled to Amazon-fulfilled as the tool gives you a detailed comparison of costs and profits for each model.

There are various components of Amazon fees, and it's good to know if the calculator considers them all or includes only a few of them. The calculator includes:

- o Fees for selling on Amazon – This component consists of two different fees— referral fees and variable closing fees. While the referral fee is the cost of selling an item on Amazon, variable closing fees are applicable only for media items (as discussed in the FBA Fee structure).

o FBA fees – The Fulfillment by FBA Fee is calculated based on the given weight and dimension of the product. As discussed in a previous section, this consists of two components—a monthly storage fee and a fulfillment fee. While the fulfillment fee is for the cost of picking, packing and shipping to the customer and customer service, the monthly storage fee is based on the volume of product.

Now that you know what's included in the FBA calculator and what isn't, let's look at an example using a yoga mat.

The first step is to provide the calculator with a unique identifier that pulls up your product. You can use an EAN, ASIN or just use the search term.

Once you've looked up the product, start feeding the values into the fields in FBA to calculate the profit margin. You need to enter the item price—to enter this, you can research similar products and play around with the price to see what kind of profit you can get by lowering or raising the price. For our example, let's use the sale price of $12.

The next field that needs to be entered is the Ship to Amazon field.

If you've been selling your products on Amazon, you might know the average price of shipping the products to Amazon generally depends on the dimensions of the product and the quantity. Enter random values and play around with the price to see what the profit margin will be. You can even leave this blank, but remember that this is going to impact your total costs and profit margin.

For our example, let us keep the Ship to Amazon cost at $0.30 per a unit. The last field you need to enter is the Cost of Product field—the cost to buy one unit from your manufacturer. Note that this should include all the costs you would pay for the product, overseas shipping costs, packaging material and other expenses. This should be the "total" cost. For our example, let us consider the Cost of Product to be $2.50.

Once you have entered values in all the fields, click on the Calculate tab and you will be provided with the total profit/total margin for the product, based on the values you entered in the fields, as well as the Selling on Amazon fees and FBA fees.

To analyze the various attributes involved, the calculator also creates several graphs on the right-hand side of the screen offering you a visual display of your cost, net profit, margin and so on.

FBA Global Selling

Amazon lets you sell your products not just in your country but globally to customers in more than 180 countries. Follow the same steps for listing your product as with local/national sales, as discussed previously.

There are certain products that are banned in specific regions. For instance, watches, clothing, accessories, beauty products, etc. cannot be sold on Amazon Japan.

Currently, Amazon has 11 marketplaces, allowing its sellers to grow their businesses and sell internationally.

- North America – United States (Amazon.com); Canada (Amazon.ca);Mexico (Amazon.com.mx)
- Europe – United Kingdom (Amazon.uk); Germany, Italy, Spain and France
- Asia – China (Amazon.cn); Japan (Amazon.jp); and India (Amazon.in)

These marketplaces represent some of the world's largest selling opportunities. One of the biggest advantages is that sellers, no matter how big or small, can leverage the power of Amazon to build their business in the international market without having to pay any upfront costs. Amazon takes care of everything—packing, shipping, etc. across the globe without you having to bother about customs or selling rules. For example, you can ship your products to the fulfillment center in the UK, and a customer in Europe can have that item shipped to them directly.

The rules and requirements are slightly different based on your region. Therefore, you need to be aware of all rules and policies before starting your business. Even the fees of products vary based on the marketplace. So, let us look at what Amazon has to offer its sellers so that they can enter marketplaces and expand their businesses internationally.

Access the International Market: Amazon's Global Selling offers its sellers access to the international marketplaces of North America, Asia and Europe. But the market reach is not limited to just these regions.

The products can be bought by consumers in 180 countries. Businesses benefit from the trust and value Amazon has built over the years.

European Marketplaces: If a seller already has an account in any one of the European marketplaces and is looking to expand his business in another marketplace within Europe, the Amazon Europe Marketplaces feature allows its sellers to expand their business within Europe without having to create separate accounts for a new region. The Building International Listing feature lets sellers manage product listings across Europe through a single primary European account. This also takes care of the changes in listings and pricing because when the attributes change in the primary account, the changes are automatically reflected in other European accounts.

Currency Converter for Global Sellers: To handle the payments for global selling, Amazon offers a Currency Converter to its sellers. This tool allows global sellers to receive payments for their products in their local currency, in their local bank account. The currency conversion rate is included in the tool and using this rate, the payment is converted to the local currency and deposited to the local bank account of the seller. The Currency Converter is available only for sellers who have a bank account in one of ten international countries and for currencies supported by the Amazon Currency Conversion for Sellers tool.

Global Selling by Amazon: When sellers choose to sell their products on Amazon, they have two options to fulfill their orders. They can either do it on their own or use the FBA service. If they decide to do it on their own, they're responsible for handling all orders, customs, import taxes, picking and packing, returns and so on. If they choose to use FBA, most challenges are handled by Amazon, which includes picking and packing of the items, managing inventory, shipping the products to the customers and so on. As per this program, sellers are required to store their inventory at the fulfillment centers. For sellers trying to sell their items in Amazon European Marketplaces, there are two options available for fulfillment—the European Fulfillment Network (EFN) and the Multi-Country Inventory Fulfillment Network (MFN).

- The EFN allows sellers to send their complete inventory to a fulfillment center located in a primary source country. When customers place an order from anywhere in Europe, the order is fulfilled from the primary location. This simplifies the process and hence is recommended for all new businesses in Europe.
- The MFN gives the sellers an option to store their inventory in different centers in Europe. This helps businesses store their products strategically, depending on the demands of their customers.

Amazon has divided its sellers into groups based on their location. Depending on the group you belong to, below are the steps you must follow to set up your seller account.

Group 1: Seller is based in the US.

The seller needs to set up an Amazon Seller central account by keying in all the required business and personal details.

Group 2: Seller operates from a country that is supported.

The seller needs to create a seller account by keying in all the required details.

Group 3: Seller operates from a country that is not supported, but the seller is allowed to do business on the platform.

The seller needs to create a Payoneer account to receive and send payments to and from his account. Next, he should set up an Amazon Seller Account by keying in all the required details.

Group 4: Seller operates out of a country that is not supported.

In this case, the seller can either get a local residential address in a country that is supported by the platform and then set up the account depending on the group that country belongs to, or he can get connected with a local person from a country that is allowed to sell on the platform.

US Tax Requirements for UK Sellers

Many sellers operating from the UK buy their private label products manufactured in China and list them on Amazon UK. FBA makes it really easy for sellers who want to grow their brand to expand internationally. Since each country has its own set of laws and policies when it comes to selling online, it is important to know and gather all the information needed to set up and start a business in another country. Particularly, when it comes to tax requirements, you might struggle to get all the required information online.

In the UK, Private Limited companies that sell their products on Amazon.com need to file annual tax returns and pay on their profits. In the US, partnerships and corporations that sell products on Amazon.com need to file annual accounts and pay federal taxes.

In the UK, LTD companies that do business with Amazon UK and have a turnover of more than a defined amount over a period of 12 months need to pay VAT on the sales they make. In the US, sellers who do business on Amazon.com collect sales tax in the states (tax rate and policies are different for each state) where they store and sell their inventory.

UK sellers need to pay sales tax as well as a tax on the profits they make by selling on Amazon.com and using FBA. If they are using FBA, they owe tax on the sales in multiple states.

The tax treaty between the US and the UK prevents sellers from paying double taxes on the profits they make on their products depending on the structure of their company. The treaty prevents businesses from paying taxes on their sales in the US when they are paying them in the UK. All businesses that benefit from this treaty still file tax returns, but it's only paperwork, and no payment is needed.

Chapter 2 – Product Research

Amazon sells millions of products each day, so you can imagine the number of opportunities it offers to its sellers as well as buyers. Sourcing an item is all about finding the right opportunities. It's about looking for products that are popular in the market, but are still not available that easily to the customers. To become successful on Amazon, you need to find what things people are searching for on Amazon. This chapter will cover the most important part of being a seller on Amazon—finding profitable products that can be sold on Amazon platform and produce good revenue. The product you choose is going to determine everything about your business. That's why it is crucial that you spend a lot of time thinking and finding what you want to sell.

Before we dive deeper into our product research, let us first try to understand the basics of this entire process so that we have a clear picture of what you are going to do and how to do it effectively.

Know What You are Doing

To become successful in business, it is very important to know what you are attempting to do. You are either trying to sell unwanted items around your house, or you are trying to buy an item cheaply and then sell it under your own brand. This certainly is not retail arbitrage where people visit various stores to find underpriced items to sell them on Amazon for a profit. You are trying to find items that can be sourced from China for lower prices and then be private labeled under your brand. After branding, these items can be sold on Amazon. This is legit, unlike retail arbitrage.

Look for things that are in high demand, but less visible. These items can come from anywhere—from around you, or from the discussions you have with your friends and relatives. The best approach to understanding what to sell on Amazon is to look for products that are doing well in the market and then sell them yourself with a modification, adding your brand.

There are some strategies that you can follow in order to find items that can generate a good profit margin on Amazon. Your product:

- should have an average product sale price of $10 - $40
- shouldn't have any brand names within that niche or product category
- should encourage multiple, recurring purchases
- should be lightweight, preferably less than two pounds
- shouldn't be fragile
- should be easily outsourced for manufacture in China
- should be manufactured for a price that is at least 25% lesser than the sale price
- should be ever-green, not a seasonal product
- should have consistent sales
- should have enough room for optimization/improvement under the current listing

- should be superior to many similar products available in the market
- should be similar to only 4-5 similar products with less than 100 reviews.
- should have top three keywords used in monthly product searches (more than 100,000)
- Similar products with a 5000 Best Seller Rank or Lower in the main category.
- Similar products doing well on other websites, such as eBay

Requirements for Product Search

Average Product Sale Price of $10 - $40 – The selling price of an item is one of the most important decisions you must make before placing an order. This price range is appropriate for product pricing because most people make buying decisions for products that fall in this range. If an item is priced in this range, shoppers do not spend more time researching other products before making their decision as they feel this price is low enough that they can risk the product not being profitable. Think of it this way—how much research do people do before buying an electronic gadget that is worth thousands of dollars? On the other hand, how much research is involved buying a small USB device that is worth $20? People do not spend too much of their precious time in buying items that are inexpensive. Think about the complexity of a television set—many parts inside, therefore, expensive. Now think about a USB drive—simple product, nothing complicated, therefore, inexpensive.

The last reason items in this price range are preferred is because items in this range allow for a lower barrier to enter the market. Let's look at it this way:

- Product xyz is being sold for $20 and you can get it made in China for $3. So, for 100 items, it will cost you $300 without shipping costs.
- Product abc is being sold for $99 and you can get it made in China for $22 per unit. So, for 100 items, it will cost you $2200 without shipping costs.

Even in terms of inventory, it is better to have inexpensive products so that you can avoid paying thousands of dollars for inventory.

No brand names within that niche or product category – There shouldn't be brand names in the same product category you are trying to sell your product. You want to compete with weak, non-branded products that do not carry any name on their own. Staying away from brands helps shoppers make buying decisions because when they are choosing between products, they will prefer a brand they know instead of something they do not know. Hence, having no other brands in that niche is good for you to enter the marketplace. A good way to check whether there are brands that dominate the product category is to look for that product category on Amazon and see if you find any known brands in the listings. If you can spot known brands on the first page, you might not want to choose that product. But if it's not exactly like your product, having a brand on the first page is okay.

In an ideal scenario, you want every listing on the first page of the product search to have a different brand—a no-name brand. Finding a product without a brand dominating the marketplace is crucial for making good sales as it becomes difficult when you have to compete for your survival in the market, which is full of well-known brands.

Encourages multiple, recurring purchases – An added bonus to your sales is if you choose a product that encourages recurring purchases. Consider a protein supplement that requires multiple, recurring purchases since the buyer will run out after a while. The negative to this is that a product which encourages recurring purchases generally has good competition.

Items should be lightweight – Choose products that are lightweight, preferably anything less than two to three pounds. More than three pounds is considered heavy. This weight denotes the shipping weight of one unit, which includes the item itself, packaging, as well as the shipping box. The best way to determine an estimated weight of your item is to find similar products on Amazon. Let's say you are planning to sell a dog toy. Search for dog toys on Amazon and find something similar to your product. Now scroll down on the product page to find the Product Details and look for its shipping weight.

Shipping weight is important because the shipping quotation you are going to get from your supplier depends on this weight. The lighter the item, the less the shipping cost, which implies more profit margin. That's what your aim is! The weight of the product also has a role to play in the Amazon fees. Amazon charges around $2 for anything that weighs less than two pounds and then for each additional pound, Amazon charges extra. If your product weighs five pounds, it will be charged $2 + (extra charge * 3) for a unit—just for the weight-handling fees. Weight plays a key role in your profit margin. So, keep it as light as possible.

Should not be fragile – The best way to ensure this is to look for products that are not delicate. Some good examples of such products are exercising mats and door mats, etc. If you look at these products, they have only one part. By choosing a simple product, you can easily find an inexpensive supplier to manufacture it. Always choose products that are: easy to be made, durable, generic, which do not have moving parts or contain electronic parts and are designed to do just one job.

Less than 100 reviews – Always try to look for clues in the Reviews for Competitor Analysis. To search for profitable products sold on Amazon, Jungle Scout and other tools, analyze top listings for a keyword. It scans the product catalogue on Amazon instantly so you can save time in researching and invest that time instead into your business. In terms of competition, the aim is to find top results from this listing that have less than 100-200 reviews. If not, look for items with up to 500 reviews. More reviews mean tougher competition, which implies spending more time and money to compete. Items with less than 100 reviews are considered easy to beat.

5000 Best Seller Rank or Lower – Analyze the demand by using the estimated sales or the Best Seller Rank. The Best Seller Rank is an indicator that tells you how well a product is selling within its category. For example, a product that has a BSR of 10,000 is not selling as much as another product in the same category with BSR 1000. This is a useful indicator because as a seller you want to know if there is a demand for the product or not.

To determine this rank, click on the listing and scroll down to the product detail section. There you will see the product rank which Amazon gives to each of its products. The higher the rank, the fewer sales for that listing. With the help of the Sales Estimator tool on Amazon, use this rank to determine the monthly sales of that product. Do this for all the top 10 listings for the searched keyword. If the product is making an average sale of 300 per month, or 10 per day, it's good to go, but if the sales are less than 10 per day, the product doesn't seem to be in much demand in the market.

Next, check the depth of the market, which means how the sales of a product are spread out in the market. If most of the sales are made by the top one or two listings of that product, it means you will have to be the best to sell that item in the market, as the sales are not uniformly distributed.

Each product on Amazon belongs to a category. The main category would be something like Home Décor, while a sub-category would be Living Room Décor. When it comes to the Best Seller Rank, the main category is more important, as a lower Seller Rank in the main category means it is doing well in the market.

At least 25% less than the Selling Price – If the manufacturing cost of a product is such that it is at least 25 percent less than the cost at which it can be sold, it's a good candidate for a product possibly capable of generating a profit margin. You can do research on your product on various websites including Alibaba to check for the price at which suppliers are making this product. On these websites, suppliers give you an estimated price per unit. Once you know the estimated cost, you can check whether it fulfills your criteria.

Don't forget that there will be shipping costs, Amazon selling costs and FBA fees, apart from the manufacturing costs. After taking into account all of these, you should still have a sufficient profit margin.

Room for Optimization and Improvement – There are times when the listings appearing on the first page are not optimized, and there is room for improvement. This can include weak product descriptions, low-quality images of the product, no image or single images, missing important details, missing or non-catchy headlines and so on. Irrespective of all this, if the listing has still made it to the top, it means the market for this product is big and the competition is weak. If you come up with something similar that is better optimized, it will be easy to reach the top of the chart.

Superior to similar products – If you see a listing which you feel can be improved and optimized to sell better, it has a chance to have a good market and sales. To be able to come up with a superior market, look at the shortcomings of existing listings, what they lack and how they can be improved. This will give you an idea of how to display a product that has an advantage over similar products in the market.

How to make better products? See what you can do that your competitors are not doing. For instance, say you're looking at a baking mat and wish to sell something similar that sets it apart from every other mat on the market. After some research, you might find that, per the reviews, all baking mats are really small and customers are looking for something bigger. You then know you need to find a slightly bigger baking mat that has all other features too.

Manufactured in China – To be able to get the product made in China is important because China can give you quality, inexpensive products. Search for your product on Alibaba and see if you can find similar products. If you come across a couple of suppliers who are making similar products, you can assume it can be made.

Several monthly searches – Check whether the top three product keywords have several (more than 100,000) monthly searches because this means the market for the product is huge.

Similar products doing well on other websites – Identifying niche websites that are doing well in the marketplace is another great way of uncovering opportunities for fast-moving, profitable products. These days, there are several sites like Flippa, which buy and sell websites, which you can use to search for niches. To find a niche, you can find key information on these sites such as the traffic, monetization figures and so on. You can filter the sites that monetize well on Amazon, which means there is a high chance of an associated high demand product for this site. Find these related products and then check out the listings for the product on Amazon. If similar products are doing well on other websites, it can be assumed that the market for that product/niche is big. It's always a good sign to know that there is a demand for the product you have chosen for your business.

You can cycle through the entire process of finding profitable niches and then cherry-pick the bestselling products. See if the listings for this product have any opportunity on Amazon. If not, you can take some time to determine more details for these niches, look for more related information and ideas and then find the associated products and listings.

An ever-green product – As discussed before, the next factor to consider while searching for a profitable product is seasonality. You might look at all those plum cakes lying in almost all the bakeries in your area during the months of November, December and January. The sales of this product are more than 6000 items per month. But what about sales after January? There's probably a steep drop.

Ensuring sales are consistent – You've analyzed the top listings for a product and have evaluated the competition levels as well as sales for these listings. It all looks great. Now, the next step is to verify the sales to ensure the numbers are consistent over time. This is important because you certainly do not want to decide to sell a particular product by assuming it is going to be a good business and profit margin if it just happened to do well by chance one day. So, there is a need to monitor the results over a period of time, at least for two to three weeks. Use the estimate tool and note the estimates for each of those days to see if the results are consistent. If there are fluctuations, how much do they change? If you see a huge difference, there is an issue, but if the sales are around 3000 units per month and then around 2000 units for six-seven days, it shows the sales are consistent.

How to do the Real Job

Use the Product Research Tools

Choosing a product can make or break your business. The good news for all FBA sellers is that they can leverage the power of Product Search tools, such as Jungle Scout, to find profitable ideas and get estimates and sales. However, all this does take time—time to search products, time to promote products and time to increase sales. Let's look at some of the tools that can help you make your job easier.

Jungle Scout

Greg Mercer came up with the amazing web app known as Jungle Scout which offers users a custom filter system for searching profitable niches/products and related information about these products. It helps businesses find opportunities that are backed by the most reliable database, which prevents expensive mistakes. Jungle Scout offers its users the following:

- A WebApp that helps users scan Amazon's spectrum of products to find what's hot in the market.
- A suite of three tools: an Amazon database for sellers, the niche hunter and a product tracker, which, together, filter the products that meet your criteria.
- Chrome Extension, a real-time fast checker that compares your ideas against the sales data so that you know what the best products are statistically.

While the WebApp is a powerful tool that runs on your website, the Chrome Extension works on the data pulled from the web sources, for instance, estimated revenue, etc.

Jungle Scout finds products that are in demand but have low competition/reviews in the market. To effectively utilize it:

1. Find the Best Seller listing for any product on Amazon, ensuring you use the main category of the chosen product.
2. Enter the rank of those listings in the Jungle Scout tool and find the most up-to-date and accurate estimates.
3. Browse through Jungle Scout's WebApp catalog, which offers some of the bestselling products on Amazon categorized by Best Seller Rank, number of reviews, monthly and daily sales,

price and so on. The app filters the ideas based on your criteria and shows you the shortlisted listings. Where Amazon's current catalogue is designed to make shopping an easy and fun-filled task for shoppers, the WebApp is specifically designed for sellers to filter data based on criteria helpful to them. For instance, you can apply some available filters like price between $30 and $40, sales of at least 400 units per month and fewer reviews than 50 (an attribute that shows the product is not too competitive).

For this list, the task is to find products that are doing well in terms of sales. Certain things that you should avoid while searching the product/niche are:

- potential liabilities
- checking clothing and licensed brands
- fragile items
- anything that can stop working at any point in time, in order to prevent bad customer reviews

Jungle Scout offers additional filters that share results by digging deeper into the statistical data. These filters are:

1) **Search products that have poor ratings** – With the help of a customer filter such as "how the heck do they sell so well with a crap product," one can find products that are doing well in the marketplace but have poor ratings, meaning below 3.2. These are the products that have the potential for improvement; their

quality or any other shortcoming can be improved by investigating their customer reviews. If we go through the bad reviews and work on making the product better, the product might start receiving positive reviews and that will make a difference in the numbers. Addressing these shortcomings can turn into a great opportunity for sellers!

2) **Look for products that sell well despite their bad ratings** – With the help of a filter, Jungle Scout points out all the products that are doing well in the market despite having poor product ratings. The Listing Score on the app rates the products based on their quality, the strength of rating, features and so on.

These filters offer opportunities to find additional ideas for product searches. What once used to be a challenge of deadly data accumulation is now the issue of data overload. Nevertheless, understand that there is nothing like "too much data" even if it might be confusing for many sellers to know how to filter and interpret the numbers. Should the data be prioritized on the basis of the number of reviews or for items by FBA sellers only? What is the comfortable spot between sufficient product demand and too much competition in the marketplace? Let's look at some general guidelines to parse through the data filtered by Jungle Scout, although these might not be followed strictly under all types of situations. You can always tailor them to your marketing investment, tolerance for competition and the category you are targeting. Certainly, there is no guarantee that the shortlisted product is going to fetch you enough profit margins regardless of how promising the numbers are or how much data you have collected. The only way to know is to get started!

Is There Enough Demand for the Product?

As a seller, you would like to see at least 300-400 units being sold per month. The logic is that there should be at least 10-12 units sold per day.

Is There Enough Room for the Product at the Top?

Competition is always subjective, depending on how much time and money you are looking to invest. Generally, sellers like to see a product in the top 10 with less than 100 reviews. For them, it is a good indication that the listing can rank well in a short span of time. However, track the organic ranking of the product over a span of time.

Is the Brand Dominance Big?

Having big brand dominance is okay if there is no other bad news for the product. There are two reasons for this. Firstly, you can always make optimizations to the listing to capture some of the demands of the consumers where the big brands cannot, and secondly, product positioning can be altered to your advantage so that you can highlight all that customers like in the big brand while still presenting your product in a different manner—low priced, better quality and better customer guided.

Jungle Scout could very well be your secret weapon to make smarter business decisions and outpace competitors.

Google Trends

Whether it is finding profitable niches/products to sell on e-commerce sites or discovering content ideas, the potential of Google Trends is unbeatable. Google Trends is a free tool offered by Google that helps you make comparisons between various trends and search items. Equipped with multiple features, this tool gives you the potential to find the most happening trends of today and tomorrow. This tool is easy to use. Just browse through the website and check the various options available on the dashboard. From the dashboard, you can navigate to different topics and find out what's trending in the marketplaces today. Just enter what you are looking for in the search area and get started!

Understand what your potential customers are looking for. With its vast range of features, Google is more than just a search engine. It has become the reflection of what people are looking for—an indicative tool that mirrors their interests and opinion. Whether you're into fashion or finance, it can benefit you by helping you understand the interests of the audiences in your industry.

Just enter the keyword you have chosen in the search area and begin the search. You'll see a graph that highlights the search trends in your domain over time, comparing the stats for the keyword over time. You can also analyze the results for your specific region.

Use Google Trends to:

- Find products for your business – You can use Trends to help you generate ideas for products that you can sell. It can tell you if the product you are considering will actually do well by researching past demands and providing similar product lines. Suppose you want to set up a business selling virtual reality gadgets in Europe. Enter some keywords related to the product into Google Trends and view the data from Europe over the last three or four years. The graph will show you how it has been doing over a span of time and how it is doing currently. If it has been moving upward recently, this might be an indication that the product will continue to become popular in the upcoming months and can be considered a good investment for your business. You can also identify the seasonality of the product by the peaks in the graph. If the graph shows spikes around a specific month and low volume during rest of the year, it can be considered a seasonal product. You can take your research further by using the Related Topics option on Trends to dig deeper into the product.
- Analyze and monitor how your competitors and you are performing in the marketplace. The News Headlines feature of Trends lets you do this in conjunction with positive and negative stories. If you search for a competitor selling a similar product and his graph looks low throughout years and then suddenly spikes, you

might wonder how it managed to become that popular. News Headlines will help you understand these peaks. Just select the News Headlines checkbox, and you will learn how and why these peaks develop.

CamelCamelCamel & Keepa for Amazon FBA

CamelCamelCamel (CCC) is a free Chrome Extension that helps users make the best buying decisions. Therefore, it is one of the most important tools for any FBA seller. Why? It helps you track prices, price drops, sales rankings, community deals and a lot of other things around Amazon Product Listings. Keepa is another Chrome Extension that helps find you the best buying deals by providing price history, price fluctuations, daily watches and so on for Amazon listings.

Both these extensions are quite similar to each other in their concept but differ from each other in the actual nuts and bolts. They both use color-coded graphs to extract information, but the kind of information you get from each might not be the same. For this reason, Amazon FBA sellers choose to use both of them. Here's how each of these extensions works in detail:

CamelCamelCamel:

- Provides price history graph that can be configured to give price history of one month, six months and more.
- Provides price history from Amazon or other third-party sellers by adjusting the slide bar.

Provides sales ranking graph that helps identify products that did well in the previous months, this month, etc.

Look at the sales numbers if the graphs confuse you— the lower the rank, the higher the sales.

Keepa:

- Color graphs where orange stands for Amazon, blue for new listings, black for used items and green for the product sales rank.
- Product history that is more instinctual than CamelCamelCamel's. Unlike CCC, that gives you longer time frames, Keepa gives you more intuitive results in terms of a week, month, etc.
- Products' monetary history sorted in descending order, with low dollar amounts at the bottom and high amounts at the top.
- Product sales rank in descending order of number, with highest sales at the top and lowest at the bottom.
- In-stock and out-of-stock history of products.
- Sales rank history indicated with the help of a green line on the graph for a chosen range.

Understanding CamelCamelCamel Graphs:

If you have a chance to look at a CCC graph, it looks more like the result of a lie detector test than a graph that shows price vs. sales rank. If you read it carefully, however, it will give you important insights for your Amazon FBA business. The first and most important thing you should consider while reading a CCC graph is that you shouldn't make any key business decisions based on just the price and sales rank of a product today; you must also consider the historical data of that product.

Look at the CCC price history graph, which is the first thing that comes up whenever you search for an item on CCC. You can see the range of prices at which the item is offered on Amazon on the left, and a range of dates along the bottom of the graph. Toward the right, there is a slider which can be used to adjust the date range to one month, three months, six months, etc. You can also select or change the price type for the graph and select Amazon (green), third-party new (blue) or third-party used (red).

After the history price graph, look at the sales rank graph for the product. You can view both the graphs side by side by toggling between the two tabs—Price History and Sales Rank. The Sales Rank graph gives you the sales rank information for the different ranges. If you look at this graph, you will still see the date ranges along the bottom. However, the left side of the graph now shows the sales range instead of a range of prices of the product. The lower sales ranks are at the top and the higher ones are toward the bottom, on the left pane of the graph. Again, with the slider bar on the right-hand side, you can adjust the date ranges for the graph.

An important feature of the Sales Rank graph is that it lets you count the number of sales for a product during a chosen range of time. If there is a sharp rise in the graph, it indicates a sale. A lower sales rank (meaning a lower number such as 1, 2, or 3) implies more sales of the product. This is why the "number 1 best seller" would have a lot more sales than the "number 5 best seller".

While reading the graph from left to right, if you come across any sharp uptick, it means sales have occurred. If the line has a sharp uptick, it means more than one sale took place.

If you're trying to make a business decision about your Amazon inventory, use the historical sales rank as well as pricing data information from CamelCamelCamel graphs.

Alibaba Listings

The underlying process is similar to Jungle Scout, but Alibaba has millions of different products that you might not find on any other site. To get started, browse through the Products page of the Alibaba website and you will be greeted by a page that contains several product categories. Go through each of these categories and look for something that catches your attention. Some of the best categories on the Product page are Gifts, Sports and Toys; Home, Lights and Construction; Bags, Shoes and Accessories; Health and Beauty.

Click on the sub-category, and that will take you to a home page for all the products under that sub-category. If you look through this page, you will come across various product ideas, such as Week's Best Performing products, Most Popular products, Hot Products for the month and so on. It also offers you a filter that shows what Buyers are Searching For, followed by the categories that are most searched by the shoppers. This will give you some of the great ideas for your product for each category.

Google Keyword Planner

Google Keyword Planner is another great way to find some product ideas. First, look through Amazon's Best Sellers page and then click on a category of your choice. Once you click on a category, you will be shown a list of sub-categories on the left-hand side. Now plug in each of these sub-categories into the Google Planner. Back to Google Keyword Planner—plug in one of the shortlisted sub-categories in the search bar, and you will see all the information pop up. There are too many possible products to search through by scrolling up and down. Also, take a look at the related keywords and ad groups. These keywords and groups will help you curate ideas to find your product. If any catch your eye, check all the details about that product on Amazon.

Product Bundling Strategy

While private labeling is at the top of any retail business, it is difficult for the small businessman. Why? Because:

- importing and getting the products manufactured is not easy.
- it always requires new products.
- it requires investing thousands of dollars for the entire process.
- logo creation, branding and packaging are required.
- it's a long and time-consuming process.

A better option for those who can't opt for private labeling is product bundling. Product bundling, also known as a poor seller's private label, is the process of putting together complementary products in packages and selling them as a package for a better, faster and more convenient customer experience. The beauty of these bundles created by sellers is that they are composed of different products that are combined together to create a new product for the Amazon catalogue—a bundled product. These convenient, well-designed bundles add value to the buyers, are less expensive and are an alternative to private labeling. The concept of product bundling is similar to you putting together different products into one package and making it your own. This requires no long lead times, no importing and not too much money, but still boosts your profit margins and sales.

All you need to do to create these beautiful packages is to follow Amazon's Product Bundling policies:

- DO NOT list bundled products in which the primary product is from the Video Games category or is a video, music, book or DVD.
- Products from the Video Games category or videos, books or DVDs can be included as secondary products in a bundled product if they are somehow related and complementary to the primary product. For instance, a bundled product can consist of a skipping rope (as a primary product) and a weight loss book (as a secondary product).

- The referral fee applicable to the primary product category is applicable for the bundled product.
- All the products within the bundled product should adhere to Amazon's listing policies.
- The description and images for the bundled product should adhere to Amazon's listing policies.
- If any of the products contained in the bundle, or the bundle itself, don't adhere to the listing policies of Amazon, the product can be removed from Amazon and/or the account can be suspended. This is because Amazon holds the right to remove any product from the listing without any prior notice.

Bundle Guidelines:

- The bundled product must be comprised of items that complement each other, which means one item within the bundle should enhance the value of another item within the bundle so that it adds to convenience for the buyer.
- All the single items within the bundle are identified by a unique identification number known as ASIN/UPC, but all the items contained are sold together as a single bundled unit. A pre-packed bundle with multiple items identified by a single unique ASIN/UPC is not considered a bundled product.
- The bundled product might be listed in a single category even though the items within the bundle belong to different categories. If the

bundle has items from various categories, it might be listed under the category of the highest priced item of the bundle. Only in the case where the highest priced item in the bundle is BMVD or belongs to the Video Games category, will the bundle not be listed under the category of the highest priced item. In such cases, the bundle is listed under the category of the second highest priced item in the bundle.

- The bundle should have its own manufacturer part number or product identifier because the unique identifier of any one item in the bundle cannot serve as a unique identifier for the complete bundle. This is because using the ASIN/UPC of any one of the items in the bundle to uniquely identify the bundle is against Amazon's listing policies and can lead to the removal of the listing. One must keep the unique identifiers for the contained items and the bundle separate and unique.

- Never include generic products in the bundle as this might mislead shoppers by making them think that the generic product included in the bundle also belongs to one of the brands of the branded items in the bundle. Generic products are the items that are not associated with any brand whatsoever.

- If an item contains multiple units, for instance, four pairs of socks, it is considered as a single product and not a bundle. It should use UPCs that are applicable for multi-packs.

- If an item is a variation of another item, it should be listed as a variation within the main family of the parent product, and not as a bundle. For such cases, the Parent-Child Variations guidelines are applicable.

- If a new bundle is matched to an existing bundle product, the items present in the new bundle should be exactly the same as the items present in the existing bundle product. If the new bundle is different, even slightly, it must be created as a new listing. You cannot touch the existing bundle listing to match the specifications of the newly created bundle product.
- Once a bundle product is created, its components cannot be modified. If the items within the bundle need to be removed, or new ones are to be added, a new bundle listing must be created with a unique identifier or it should match an existing bundle listing (if the modified bundle is identical in all ways).

The pros of Amazon Product Bundling are many. If you feel you have certain items in your inventory that are not moving, bundling the ones that complement each other can be the winning ticket. Think about a seller whose listings are all about yoga—yoga mats, yoga videos, yoga eBooks and so on. The seller might not be able to sell these yoga mats along with the videos. In order to boost the sales of these underperforming products, the seller can bundle them together and create a unique bundle product comprised of the yoga mat, yoga eBook and yoga video. Buyers might love the combo. Bundled products not only add value for shoppers, they offer a unique way for sellers to reduce their competition in the marketplace.

Amazon Pricing Registry

Once you decide to launch your product on Amazon, you are likely to spend a lot of time researching every attribute and aspect of the product so that you know it inside and out. What color should it be? What dimensions are suitable? How should the packaging look? What attributes should it have? All these points are important as they govern the success of your product in the marketplace. An important thing about your product that can get it noticed is the Price. How much you sell your product for plays a key role because:

- **It impacts Sales**: If you choose to price your products too high as compared to other similar products in the marketplace, you might discourage potential customers, ultimately resulting in fewer sales.
- **It affects the Profit Margin:** Keeping the price too low will impact your profit margin and, ultimately, your business growth.
- **It increases Storage Fees:** It the product price is too high, and you do not get orders, your product will just be lying in the Amazon warehouse. You will end up paying more storage fees if you do not strategize the pricing properly.

Pricing plays an important role in your business, and you need to price your products in a way that is neither too high nor too low. Remember, this is not just a one-time job: always keep an eye on the market and update your pricing accordingly so that you remain competitive.

Let us now look at some of the strategies for pricing your products effectively.

Pricing Strategies

When you want to strategize pricing, you should look at different sources and factors that can impact your business. Particularly, you should bear in mind the business model you are using as the strategies are different when deciding prices for private labeled products vs. wholesale products.

- **Pricing Strategies for Wholesale Products/Retail Arbitrage** – The "Buy Box" is basically the word used to identify the area near the Add to Cart button. Only one seller can link his or her product directly to the Buy Box at one time. If you are a wholesale business, you are competing with similar products that exist in the market as well as other sellers for that specific Buy Box. When deciding who should win the Buy Box, pricing is one of the key factors to consider. The price needs to be competitive if you want to be successful. Keep an eye on other competitors by using various resources available with your Amazon Seller Account, such as the Manage Pricing tab, Pricing Dashboard and so on. Also look for various opportunities that help you remain competitive in the marketplace.

An important thing to remember in wholesale or retail arbitrage is the need to determine the absolute lowest price for a similar product you sell. While you should price your product in a way that you remain competitive in the market, you should not make it so low that your profit margin takes a big hit. So, think before you strategize.

- **Pricing Strategies for Private Labeled Products** – Unlike wholesale products or retail arbitrage, if you are private labeling products, you just have to compete with similar products in the marketplace; you do not have to worry about other sellers for the Buy Box. The only challenge you have is pricing your product in such a way that it compares to other similar products being sold in the marketplace. With private labeling, the pricing strategy not only impacts your profit margin and sales but also impacts the brand's reputation. If you price your product too low and it's not even close to the price of similar products, customers might question the quality and consider the product a cheap option. On the other hand, if you price your product much higher than other competitors, your potential customers might lose interest and look for other options.

As a brand owner, your aim should be to have a price strategy to price your product just right— not too low, not too high. Also, if your product features something that other similar products don't have, do not forget to highlight that and then mention why your product price is slightly higher than the competitors. Customers don't mind paying a few extra bucks to get some additional value. So bring that uniqueness to the table and get your product noticed!

Depending on what you are selling, you will have to identify the features your product has that other existing products lack and what it is that will help your potential customers. What is it that will make them select your product over other competitors in the market? After all, we are living in an era where uniqueness sells. Is your target audience concerned only about the looks or are they also looking for quality? Is there something that can help solve their issues? Is there something they have been looking for in the marketplace? The more questions, the better ideas you can curate. So, think and think deeper, and offer them additional benefits that justify the slightly higher price of your product.

Up to now, we have been considering the price and design of the product to stimulate more sales, but another thing that makes a difference is the product listing. How many unique keywords are in the description, how many bullets have you added, how many high-quality images? This adds additional value for the customers, and you gain an advantage over others selling similar products. Take the utmost care when listing your product on Amazon as this is also an art.

Managing Repricing

As we mentioned, strategizing product pricing is not a one-time activity; it is ongoing and should be monitored and updated regularly. If you're a business owner who is trying to compete with other sellers selling similar products, you'll need to regularly monitor your competition so that you can readjust the prices of your products in order to remain competitive. To reprice your products, you can use either of these options:

Option 1: Manually Repricing

You can manually reprice your products, which requires you to check the competition regularly and adjust your prices accordingly. This is the best option for those dealing with just a few products, who have the time to manually track the market on a regular basis.

Option 2: Using a Repricing Tool

You can use one of many repricing tools that will monitor your competitors, suggest comparative prices and automatically adjust the prices of your products. This way you don't have to invest extensive time on market surveys. This option is particularly beneficial for those who deal with many products and who may not have time to manually reprice them all in a timely fashion.

Option 3: Automating it in the Seller Central

You can also use the automated pricing tool available in Seller Central. This tool allows you to set your own rules that are then used by Amazon to automatically adjust pricing accordingly. Unlike other repricing tools that consider various other sources for comparison, this tool considers prices that are available for similar products on Amazon. This is the best option for sellers who sell only on Amazon.

Chapter 3 – Creating a Seller Account on Amazon

Amazon is a seller's best friend. As of 2015, it had over two million sellers worldwide, and this number continues to grow exponentially. Given the huge traffic to its site, Amazon works continually to keep its onboarding process simple, convenient and secure in order to cater to diverse clients and businesses in almost every part of the world.

Many of Amazon's partner sellers have reported an increase of up to 40 percent in their profits, thanks to Amazon alone. Three reasons why becoming a seller on Amazon is a very good idea:

1. **Seller Channel** – There's no need for you to create a separate website to bump up sales and attract buyers; everything you need as a seller is already fed into Amazon's program. All you need to do is create an account that suits your requirements and then manage everything from Seller Central. Some sellers may already have a basic website in place for marketing and branding purposes. And if you already have a website or a section of your website dealing exclusively with sales, then having an additional account with one of the leading e-commerce sites in the world just makes good financial sense.

2. **Customer Reach** – Amazon has incredible market penetration, thanks to its popularity and

business setup. In the United States alone in 2015, Amazon recorded 150 million unique visitors each month! In the United Kingdom, Amazon is rated as the fifth most visited website. Amazon partners with other websites to features its ads and also allows users to be guided to their website through the help of affiliate marketing/ linking-in sites. These are websites which host ads for Amazon, providing shoppers with an option to be redirected to the product on Amazon. Currently, there are approximately 145,271 such linking sites to amazon.co.uk alone!

The more such affiliate sites you have, the more prominence a website has in search engines. When you search for a product on a search engine such as Google or Bing, chances are you will find ads for Amazon displayed first. This is because of the vast number of linking-in sites which improve the website's statistics and quality of links. People tend to place their trust more easily on such reputed websites because their ads appear right at the top of the first page when they search for a product.

3. **Amazon's Brand** – According to the Nielsen Company's Harris Poll of 2016, Amazon was ranked number one in terms of reputation. This information is based on a survey which deals with the most visible companies in the US. Forbes said in one of their surveys that:

- Out of every $10 spent on online shopping, $4 is spent on Amazon.
- Online growth can be attributed 80% to Amazon.com.
- As of June 2017, there were approximately 80 million Amazon Prime members, making up 64% of the households in the country. This means that people are willing to pay to be members of an e-commerce shopping site to get better deals and quicker delivery!

These impressive numbers simply highlight the fact that the reach of Amazon in top buying countries such as the USA, the UK and even China is undeniable. There is a huge marketplace that can be tapped if you partner with Amazon whether on a large or small scale. Later in this chapter, you will learn the difference between being an individual and a professional seller.

The bottom-line is, if there are so many buyers already hooked on Amazon, there must be a decent number of sellers catering to their needs. But there are times when sellers cannot match the demands of the buyers, or the number of players keeps changing. Entering the arena will not only give you access to a larger number of customers but will also help you maximize profits when there is a holiday season and there is a short supply of the products that you are selling.

Opening a seller's account on Amazon is a pretty straightforward process. Just like opening a bank account, there are formalities to be completed and terms and conditions to be scrutinized carefully before you sign on the dotted line. This chapter aims to explain the options you have in terms of the kind of seller you can become with Amazon in order to help you take your first step toward increasing your profits.

Amazon Seller Account

As discussed earlier, you can choose between a free Individual Amazon Seller account and a paid Professional account. Many sellers are tempted to open a free account, considering that they do not want to invest too much in their business without knowing how things will turn out. Furthermore, they've likely already spent a lot of money on inventory and other things. However, here are some things you should know before making your choice:

- You can sell an unlimited number of items with a Professional account, whereas the free Individual account allows you to sell only 40 or fewer items a month.
- With the Professional Seller account, you can avoid that extra $.99 fee that you will otherwise have to pay each time you sell an item. Do not forget that this is in addition to all the other fees you will be paying, such as storage fees, shipping fees, FBA fees, etc. So, don't let this $0.99 fee eat up your profit margin, especially if the selling price of your product itself is just a few dollars.
- With a free account, there is a cap of 20 categories you can market your product under. With a Professional account, you have access to 15 extra categories as well as the 20 that are included with the original free account.

In essence, the free account is geared toward sellers who are just trying to enter the market with retail arbitrage. Although there is a monthly fee to a Professional account, if you are serious about your business, it's worth every penny.

Creating a Seller Central Account on Amazon

In order to sign up as a seller, you can either go to services.amazon.com and click on the Selling on Amazon link, or navigate to sellercentral.amazon.com and click on Selling on Amazon. Another option is to click the Sell button at the top of the Amazon.com page. While the registration process is not difficult, the process may differ between countries. For now, let's just focus on the Amazon US marketplace.

Before you start the process of creating your account, it's helpful to have the following things ready:

1) Your registered business name and contact details, such as a phone number and email address. Note: if you prefer to have a separate email address for business, you might want to use a different address than the one linked to your Amazon Prime account, which is where Amazon will send you all transaction details. Think twice before choosing an email address for your seller account.
2) An active credit card (with a valid billing address) that is globally accepted.
3) Your tax details, including your Social Security Number or Tax ID number.

Once you have all this information ready, you can proceed with the registration process for the seller's account. You will be asked to enter your business name. When considering your business name, think of who is going to pay taxes for this business. You'll enter your contact details next, and then Amazon will ask you to enter your credit card and banking information. You'll then select your type of seller account. Select FBA if you have decided to use Amazon to fulfill your orders.

The last section is tax information. The information you provide will then be verified before your account is activated. This is so that the IRS can be notified of any taxable earnings you might have through Amazon. It also allows Amazon to keep a record of its sellers.

Once you are finished, Amazon will encourage you to list the products you intend to sell. The moment you list even one single product, you become a *launched seller* on Amazon instead of just being a *registered, not launched* seller. If you continue to be a registered, not launched seller, Amazon will follow up with you through emails and encourage you to sell products. This is because if you turn a profit by selling something, Amazon makes money from the referral fees that it earns when you sell an item.

What is Seller Central? It is the space offered to Amazon users to set up their Amazon FBA business, manage orders and inventory and do a lot of other things. At Seller Central you will find links you can use to seek permission for the products that belong to (previously discussed) gated categories. While you wait for approval, you will not be able to list any products that belong to this gated category.

Now, click on the home page of Amazon's portal for sellers. You'll need to enter specific information to become a registered seller. Click on Settings on the top corner of the home page and enter the following:

- **Account Information:** This section requires your contact details. You can edit the details given by clicking on the Edit button. You can choose to use a display name that is different from your legal name.
  - Entering the correct Return Information is crucial, especially if you are going to use the FBA service to fulfill your orders. Customers can return any product to Amazon, and if you are using FBA, it can fulfill your order and send the customer's returned item to the place you have designated. There have been scenarios where small sellers have created enough inventory, but the volume generated by returns has been so much that they don't have enough space to store their items.
  - In case you want to change your credit card details in the Charge Method, note that the account might be put on hold for a period of 24 hours while your new card details are updated in the system. Because of this, whenever you change your credit card details, call customer support and request that they shorten this holding period.

- **Notification Preferences:** Amazon sends many emails to its sellers, for various purposes including a notification for each order you receive on your listings. If you wish to segregate these emails based on their subject or want to have different people look at different issues, you can set your email notification preferences. Since your inbox may already be full, you could miss out on critical report notifications that might require a call-to-action from your end. To prevent this, you can edit your specification notification settings.

- **Return Settings:** Edit the settings to best handle product returns. All FBA returns will be handled by Amazon, but returns on orders that were fulfilled by you need to have steps in place so that there is proper coordination between you (as a seller), Amazon and the customer.

- **Log-in settings**: Here, you can change your log-in details.

- **Shipping Settings**: The Shipping Settings page helps you indicate the location the products need to be shipped from, select expedited options for media items and choose if you want to ship items internationally or domestically. You can set your own rates for orders you want to fulfill yourself but bear in mind that if you set the shipping rates too high and wait times too long, it might reduce the probability that customers will select you over your competitors.

- **Gift Options**: Amazon gives you an opportunity to offer gift messaging to your customers. You will, however, need to fill in information if you wish to offer gift messaging for orders fulfilled by you. Customers like this service, but it requires adding steps to the shipping process which you may not have time for.

- **Tax Settings:** Browse through View/Edit your Tax Collection if you want to get help from a tax professional to understand what you will need to pay in state tax for orders that are shipped into the state where you (your business) physically exists. Ensure you get clarification on this, although tax nexus generally includes taxes for the state where your business stores its inventory (warehouse) or has its office. You'll need to provide your state tax ID if you want Amazon to collect taxes from you for orders that are shipped to states where you have tax nexus. If you do not have a state tax ID, get in touch with the relevant state tax authority in order to obtain it. Though Amazon can help you by collecting your taxes, it is your responsibility as a seller to pay your taxes on time. One of the common mistakes that new sellers make is not collecting taxes on their Amazon transactions, so they end up paying the taxes out of pocket.

- **User Permission Settings**: Once you give others access, they can view/edit certain sections of your Seller Central or reports. This feature is typically used when you have different people on your team taking care of your Amazon account, but do not want to give them access to your complete account. It is up to you to remove their access to Seller Central as needed.

- **Fulfillment by Amazon**: Fill out this section if you plan to use Amazon for fulfilling your orders. This information is important so that the process is in place with Amazon to send item returns back to the correct place.

- **Information and Policies:** It is important to fill out the About Seller information so that customers get acquainted with you and your business. Some high-level details of what you do and what you specialize in will really help your potential customers. Look at how other sellers describe themselves and their businesses to get ideas. Also, upload your company logo, if you have one, so that it will appear next to the company name on the product page. In this section, you can also highlight the unique characteristics of your listings. Therefore, if your products have unusual attributes or warranties, you might want to address those in the FAQ section.

Uploading High-Quality Images of Your Product

Having high-quality product images is important to ensure a listing converts. Remember that:

- You must know what kind of pictures to take
- You need to have a product on hand that can be used to take pictures
- You need an expert who knows how to take good pictures

- You need pictures taken for a low price, without compromising on quality.

Shoppers make their buying decisions largely on the basis of product images. If the product images do not depict the product in the best way possible, this not only hurts sales but also impacts the conversion rate— one of the key ranking factors on Amazon. Certainly, a product that has a nine percent conversion rate will rank higher than another one that belongs in the same category and has a three percent conversion rate. So, the higher the listing conversion rate, the higher the product ranking.

Another important point to note is the Click-Through-Rate (CTR) from the search results on Amazon. If you have high-quality images of your product, this will produce more CTR on the product, creating more sales opportunities. Here's an example. You typed "yoga mats" in the search results, and it gave you many results. The first thing you see for each listing is an image. Even if an item is ranked sixth in the search results order, if you liked the image more than what was shown for the top five results, there is a greater chance you will click through to examine the picture further. Without clicks, there are no sales. Simply put, a product with high-quality images has better chances of high CTR and conversion rates. And both these factors play a key role in making your business successful on Amazon.

There are a number of things that make an image high quality, the first being size. Size plays a key role in defining the quality of an image. An image needs to be at least 1000px by 500px in order to take advantage of the Amazon zoom feature that was discussed earlier.

Another important element that defines the quality of the image is how much space the image covers. An image that covers 85 percent of the allotted space makes images look bigger and better, which in turn improves the conversion of your listing. This is so key that if any listing doesn't follow the 85 percent rule, Amazon removes it.

Secondary images that showcase the use of products help boost listing rankings because customers like to see how, exactly, a product can be used.

Given that high-quality images are so important, knowing how to obtain them is essential.

Use freelancing websites: There are various websites such as Upwork and Fiverr that allow you to hire photographers.

Family, friends and extended network: Maybe you know someone in your family or friends circle who is really good with cameras. Explain the details of your product and ask if they can help you.

Payment Method Details

Credit Card Requirements

As previously noted, you must have a valid credit card in order to be an Amazon seller. This card should have a billing address in one of the regions accepted by Amazon. By providing Amazon with security and verification details for your card, you are authorizing them to use that information to settle any dues that exceed the available balance. Recurring failures in transactions can lead to suspension or even termination of your services. Amazon accepts the follow credit cards:

- MasterCard
- Visa
- Discover
- American Express
- JCB and
- Diners Club

Other alternative means of payment, such as gift certificates, PayPal or pre-paid cards are not accepted.

If you receive a notification message that the credit card attached to your seller's account is not valid, check the following:

- Expiration date
- Credit available
- Any limitations on mail order or Internet charges for the amount declined.

Bank Account Information

In the seller's account, you can enter/update your bank details but a business address must be included before bank information can be added. Sellers who have their bank account in a country that is supported by Amazon can have the amount credited into their account in US dollars (USD), Australian dollars (AUD), Great British pounds (GBP), Euros (EUR), Indian rupees (INR), etc.

Sellers can also check their US-based accounts to receive payment of sales on Amazon UK, Amazon France and Amazon Denmark.

Buyer-Seller Messaging Service

Sellers can send or receive emails from buyers on the Buyer-Seller Messages page. If you have chosen FBA to fulfill your orders on Amazon, you can use this messaging service to respond to specific questions from your customers as Amazon takes care of inquiries from buyers on behalf of FBA sellers. To use this service for your Amazon fulfilled orders, you need to enable it for your account. Here's how:

- Go to Settings and select FBA
- Click on the Edit button under Product Support
- Select Enable and click Update.

Some of the advantages of this service are:

- The Buyer-Seller Messaging Service masks confidential personal emails and provides security.
- Both parties can see emails from the company and the messaging service.
- It encourages buyer-seller interaction, resulting in reduced disputes.
- If there are disputes and claims, Amazon can resolve them faster and better as it has access to a 24/7 support team.

Essentially, the buyer-seller messaging service makes communication easier for both parties via encrypted email addresses. Let's say a buyer wants to contact a seller. The messaging service will create a random, encrypted email address instead of displaying the seller's actual email. The seller will receive the email through this alias email ID. The messaging service keeps track of all emails that are routed through their system.

If the seller wants to respond to the buyer and has the buyer's encrypted email address, he can communicate with him directly using his personal email address, treating the encrypted alias just like any other email address. Once this email reaches the system, a copy of the message will be saved under the Sent Items tab of the messaging page. Amazon has specific guidelines for using this messaging service.

Sellers can get in touch with their customers only to respond to queries or to complete orders, but they cannot contact them for promotional or marketing purposes. If you want to send an email to your potential customers on Amazon, your email should not contain:

- Any promotional or marketing messages
- Any links that take them to your website
- Promotional messages for other products or referrals/promotions of third-party products
- Logos of your company.

In order to contact potential customers:

- Click on the Manage Orders tab of your Account page and look for the relevant order.
- Go to the Contact Buyer column and click on the name of the buyer.

- On the next page, enter the message that you want to send to the buyer.
- Click Submit once you are finished.

If you want to contact your buyer using your personal email ID:

- Click on the Manage Orders tab of your Account page and look for the relevant order.
- Go to the Contact Buyer column and click on the name of the buyer.
- In the To field next to the buyer's name, copy the encrypted email address created by the messaging service.
- Navigate to the email application and use this copied address to send your message.

Identifying Spoof Emails

You might have seen emails from different addresses that say "Your item sold!"; "You have won!" or something similar, but when you open these emails, you realize they're spam. These emails are falsified and sent to you in an attempt to get sensitive account information. They look very similar to actual emails from Amazon, and often direct you to a link or site that looks similar to the legitimate website. When you reach the page, it might ask you for your credit card or account information. Phishers then steal this sensitive information and use it to commit fraud.

To avoid such scenarios, follow these simple rules before opening any email:

Know What Amazon Will Never Ask:

- Your Amazon account password
- Your tax identification number or Social Security Number
- Your bank account information or credit card details, your pin or security code
- Any other information that can personally identify you

Look for These Things in the Emails:

- Phishing emails are generally created by translating the content from another language, so look for grammar or other errors.
- Check the email address carefully. Genuine emails from Amazon will always have "@amazon.com" at the end. Examples of some spam email addresses include amazon-payment@payments-amazon.com
- Check the header information of the email. If the "reply to," "received from" doesn't have @amazon.com, it is not genuine.
- With most emails, you can check the source. This method depends on the header information that varies based on the email program you use.
- Check the website address as some phishers set up their accounts on spoofed websites that will have the word "Amazon" in the URL (it can be anywhere). You should know the genuine website always ends with amazon.com; there is never any other word attached, such as payment-amazon or security-amazon.

- Never follow instructions given in the spoofed email that claim to help you unsubscribe to something. Many phishers use this method to create a list of working email addresses that they can use to commit frauds.
- Use only the feature given in your seller account to track your orders. The notification emails from Amazon are an easy and useful way of following/tracking your orders. If you are confused between genuine and fraudulent emails, always go with the safer option of using the Manage Order tab of your account. Go to your Seller Account on Amazon and look for this tab. It will have up-to-date information about all your orders.
- Sometimes these phishing emails offer great deals and special offers. They ask you to do simple things to win these offers, such as logging into your seller account and thereby obtaining discounts on certain things. Know that Amazon will never ask you to log into your account by sending such mails.

So, now you know how to create an Amazon seller's account, how to set up your account and how to customize different settings to suit your needs. No matter whether you are trying to open an account on Amazon UK or Amazon US, the steps remain the same; only the bridge website changes. If you want to open an account on Amazon US, you will have to browse through amazon.com and if it is Amazon UK, you'll need to use the URL of amazon.co.uk. Everything else remains the same.

Chapter 4 – Find a Supplier to Source your Products

Now you have a product in mind that you can sell and it's time to obtain a supplier or manufacturing company that can source products at a wholesale price and brand them under your private label.

You can either source your items from another country or get them from manufacturers that operate domestically (based in the country where you operate). There are pros and cons.

The Pros of Outsourcing:

- Great item selection to choose from.
- Products can be made at very low prices.
- It is not difficult to identify a supplier who can manufacture the product you want to sell.
- Suppliers are ready to work for anyone who pays them.

The Cons of Outsourcing:

- Substantial shipping charges may be applicable.
- Customers may not understand the actual value of the product.
- Shipping increases wait time.
- There are more chances of things not going as planned, due to communication gaps.

When you evaluate both sides, you will see that sourcing products overseas seem to be a better way due to the quality of the product and the lower manufacturing costs. You can deal with the language barrier by choosing a country where people can understand your language. If you are able to find a supplier who is ready to make the product for you at competitive prices, by all means, go with that manufacturer.

Why Your Products Should Be Manufactured in China

Manufacturing your products in any other country can be really daunting due to culture and language barriers. But even then, the benefits of getting the products manufactured in China certainly overshadow these barriers. You can easily overcome the language barrier as most manufacturers (at least the famous ones, as they have to deal with English-speaking clients often) will have a representative who can speak and understand English.

Chinese manufacturing offers:

- **Better service:** This is particularly important for all beginners as initially, they will be looking at placing small orders and hence very few manufacturers will be interested in doing business with them. Chinese manufacturers, however, will.
- **Better output:** Believe it or not, there are hardly any manufacturers in China who cannot deliver what you are looking for—whether it is big or small. Also, when they commit to being ready with your order within a specific time frame, there are high chances that they will do

so. In most of the cases, local manufacturers take you for granted and ask for more time.

- **Ability to duplicate products:** Chinese manufacturers are extremely good at creating something unique from an existing idea; they do not have to start from scratch. Suppose you are manufacturing yoga mats and you really like the texture and design of xyz yoga mats available in the market. You show the product to the manufacturer and ask them to give your product the same design and texture. Trust me, you won't be disappointed when you see the results.

Now, the next question is how to find suppliers. To keep things simple and straightforward, let's consider Alibaba, which specializes in global wholesale trading of products with most of its manufacturers based in China, India and across Southeast Asia.

Sourcing Your Products using Alibaba

Alibaba, an online marketplace founded in 1999 that connects suppliers and manufacturers around the globe, is where businesses go to inexpensively source their products in bulk so that they can private label them or resell them. Alibaba first originated in China. Though it has suppliers from other parts of the world too, it is essentially China's version of Amazon.

Sellers looking to sell their products on Amazon can find virtually anything on Alibaba including apparel, kitchenware, toys and footwear. One of the biggest advantages of using Alibaba is that both sellers and buyers can browse through their huge database of manufacturers, suppliers and products.

Alibaba makes it simple for you to find suppliers who are willing to work with you quickly and efficiently to create your product. The website also helps its users by offering certain measures to ensure that you work only with trusted partners, ensuring you are never scammed.

Look for Your Product

The first step in the process of finding a supplier who can source your product is to look for your product. This should bring you to a big list of suppliers who can possibly help you make your item. Filters such as Gold Supplier, Assessed Supplier, etc. help you find only legitimate suppliers. You also have an option to filter the results based on Location and Minimum Order.

Generally, it's advisable to use the Trade Assurance and Gold Supplier filters to find authentic suppliers. However, it's helpful to understand what each of these filters does so that you can use them effectively and efficiently.

Trade Assurance_– This filter provides a free guarantee of an assessment of product quality prior to shipment as well as on-time shipment. Particularly when you have stringent deadlines, it's a useful filter, specifically designed to build trust between suppliers and buyers on Alibaba. You are covered if your products are not shipped on time or if the quality of your product does not meet the standards agreed to in the contract.

Gold Supplier – By selecting this filter, Alibaba shows only suppliers who are prequalified on the website, paying an annual fee to be tagged as Gold Suppliers. If you apply this filter while looking for suppliers, it should show you only the genuine ones, but there is a slight chance that some non-authentic suppliers could be mistagged. Therefore, it's preferable not rely on just this filter to eliminate poor suppliers—always use multiple filters along with your own knowledge.

On-site Check – This filter gives you a list of suppliers who have had their business' authenticity verified by Alibaba. If a supplier has an on-site check enabled, it means he/she is a genuine and trusted supplier.

Assessed Supplier – This filter offers the highest level of authentication that a supplier can ever attain on Alibaba. All those who have this tag have been verified by an inspection agency that has evaluated their operations in order to approve this label.

Location – This filter lets you source your product from a supplier who is located anywhere. So, you can filter out your results based on this filter. For example, some sellers on Amazon like to see if there are suppliers based in America to manufacture their product. If not, they can select another region.

Minimum Order – The Minimum Order filter lets you select the size of your minimum order. For instance, if you want the order to be less than 100, you can enter 100 in the Minimum Order box so that it lists suppliers that can give you a minimum order quantity of less than 100. This is particularly useful when you are looking only for suppliers who can give you the number of units you are looking to buy. Do not just go by the number they mention on their product page, as some of them do say they have x number as a Minimum Order Quantity, but even then they are okay to work with you based on your preferences.

Most people generally opt to use the Gold Supplier filter as it does a good job of filtering out spam. Some businesses also choose to use Trade Assurance as this is also a great filter to ensure you are dealing with only trusted suppliers. The best thing to do is to check all the filters while doing the product search for the first time. This way you are increasing the possibility of finding only legitimate supplies. Based on the type of item you have decided to sell, you might or might not find suppliers if you apply all the filters. If your product is popular among suppliers, you might see a couple of listings and you might not have too many options. If this is the case, start unchecking the filters you have applied, starting with the Assessed Supplier filter as this is the toughest one to find when it comes to suppliers.

Once you uncheck the Assessed Supplier filter, you should be able to see a good number of suppliers for your product. If you still do not see too many options, begin unchecking other filters until you find one, but try to keep the Gold Supplier filter on.

Different Sections of the Product Page

If you are using Alibaba for the first time, it's helpful to familiarize yourself with different sections on the product page.

Search Bar – This is the area where you can search for manufacturers or products you are interested in. Note: there is a drop-down box on the left side of the search bar, and here you can refine your search for Products, Quotes or Suppliers.

Sourcing Solutions – This drop-down menu offers many options to users so that they can easily refine their search. Suppliers can be efficiently searched for by submitting a buying request, region, type of stocks, global expos and so on.

Pictures – This is quite self-explanatory as it shows you images of the listed products. If there are good quality images of the product, you can see that the supplier cares enough to offer details to his customers.

Free On-Board Price – FOB, or Free on Board, gives you the cost range that is required to create one unit. Note: this price will be different from what you will be offered by the suppliers as this is just a rough estimate. After adding various components, the cost will increase.

Minimum Order Quantity (MOQ) – MOQ, or Minimum Order Quantity, gives the minimum number of units per order. For instance, with a specific brand of toy where the minimum order quantity is 1500 units, the supplier will take orders only when the minimum number is 1500. Note: although many suppliers mention a high MOQ for their orders, they may be open to lowering it if you make the request. Talk to them before making any decision.

Supply Ability – This gives you a rough estimate of how much the supplier can produce in a month. This is not that helpful as good suppliers should be able to supply as many products as you need.

Payment Options – Although there are several payment methods available, it is always good to weigh the pros and cons to understand which one works the best. Here are the most common payment methods along with information about the associated risk level for each:

- **Bank Transfer**: With bank transfers, the supplier receives the money upfront (even before production starts). This method is quite risky and is therefore not recommended for new sellers. Even if you are not new, a bank transfer is not a good option unless you know the supplier. Once the payment is made, and you are not happy with what has been delivered to you, there is little you can do about it. *Risk level: High*
- **Letter of Credit**: This is a fairly safe option and works out well for both the buyers and suppliers. However, this method involves some complex procedures and is recommended only for big orders. *Risk level: Low*
- **PayPal**: PayPal is a well-known payment method that is typically used by those who offer or receive services from individuals/companies overseas. PayPal is quite easy to use and presents a safe payment method for buyers as it has a good level of buyer protection. Although it is popular with buyers, it is not as popular

among the suppliers due to high tax rates, difficulties with withdrawals and other chargebacks from dishonest buyers. *Risk level: Fairly safe*

- **Western Union**: Western Union is seen as a risky option for buyers and is not recommended when buyers' payments are not protected through escrow. Buyers can use this if they know the sellers well, but there is no rescue for them if things do not turn out to be the way they had assumed. *Risk level: Very high*

- **Escrow**: Escrow service is offered by several companies that are ready to hold the payment for the two parties. In this payment method, a buyer's money is held by a third-party and is only transferred to the seller's account after the buyer confirms on-time and satisfactory delivery of his order. This payment method is fairly safe for both the buyer and the supplier and is recommended for online purchases. *Risk level: Low*

Categories – This menu helps users further refine their search on Alibaba according to the category they are interested in. It is a great place to search for options if you have an idea of what you are looking for and the niche market you want to check but you do not actually have any specific product in mind.

Supplier information – On the right of the product page, there appears a small section that gives useful information about a supplier, which is important before a business decision is made. It tells the name of the supplier's company, whether the individual/company is verified, how long the individual/company has been in this business, how long they have been a Gold Supplier (if they are one), what their specialties and strengths are, what are the top markets they operate in and so on. All this information comes in handy when you want to understand if they are legitimate so you can gauge their authenticity.

Product Quick Details – When you scroll down the page, you can find some of the most crucial information about the product—material, size, color, etc. By switching from Product Details tab to Company profile, you can get all the information related to the company.

AliExpress – Alibaba has a sister website, AliExpress, which is an excellent marketplace for those who are looking for a targeted consumer market and not a business market. In the last couple of years, various e-commerce businesses have started getting their products sourced from AliExpress rather than Alibaba, particularly those who want products in smaller quantities. AliExpress ships most products for free to most regions across the globe, although the shipping time is up to 30 days.

Alibaba vs. AliExpress – Alibaba and AliExpress offer two different marketplaces that cater to different types of needs and, therefore, one might be a better choice for you over the other. While Alibaba is a marketplace that connects manufacturers and business owners and is perfect for those who are looking to place bulk orders at a lower price per unit, AliExpress is a marketplace that operates at a consumer level and allows business owners to buy products in smaller quantities at a factory price per unit. If you are looking to work directly with manufacturers and create your own products, or are looking for manufacturers who specialize in a certain kind of product which you can then private label under your own brand, Alibaba should be your pick. On Alibaba, you can work directly with a manufacturer, create your own private labeled product and place bulk orders. On the other hand, buying in bulk on AliExpress isn't a good plan as it is not considered as an effective way to buy stock for your business since the prices are comparatively higher than Alibaba. If you are someone who is looking for small MOQs, AliExpress should be your pick.

Buyer Beware!

Alibaba is great—no doubt about it. But, like any company, it does have certain issues that all the customers must be aware of before reaching out to suppliers. Here are some of the issues with sourcing suppliers:

- **Middlemen**: There are thousands of manufacturers who operate on this website, and not all are real. Some are just middlemen who tend to mark up the price of products and increase the level of confusion between buyers and sellers.
- **Scammers** who loot your money: Middlemen tend to increase the price, but they only take a bit of your money. Scammers do more damage. Although Alibaba has put together many policies to ensure you deal with only legitimate suppliers, there are still some dishonest

suppliers who manage to break all the barriers and operate on Alibaba. So, you need to exercise caution, as on any platform.

- **Quality** is a subjective term: Although outsourcing overseas generally guarantees good quality, there are exceptions to every rule. Sometimes the product that sellers receive is not of high quality. Other times, there may be no intent to defraud, but your own definition of "high quality" might not match the manufacturer's.

These are a few things you can do to protect yourself and your money from bad manufacturers:

- **Verification of suppliers** – Alibaba has designed a program that includes multiple levels of verification – A&V Check, Supplier Assessment, On-site check and so on. All these checks have different badges that appear on supplier profiles and product listings as they are earned. Looking for these badges can be the first step in safeguarding yourself. There are also some third-party companies that offer to visit suppliers on your behalf to verify their identity and authenticity.
- **Look for Gold Suppliers** – All the manufacturers who are Gold Suppliers on Alibaba will bear a Gold Supplier badge on their profile/product page to let you know they have been given approval by Alibaba. They have also undergone and passed verification and authentication checks performed by third-parties. The badge provides information about

the number of years a manufacturer has been active on Alibaba, which speaks to their trustworthiness and loyalty. Remember to run multiple filters as well as looking for the Gold Supplier badge.

- **Follow up and ask questions** – As you narrow down your options, ensure you ask for a manufacturer's contact details, business license and sample products. Set up a call and do some research about them online. Remember, you are not going overboard by doing all this. Do whatever it takes to make you more confident and comfortable in your business. You can even ask manufacturers to provide a couple of images of their workplace or someone holding one of their products.

- **Ask for a sample product** – Get samples to check quality before you spend a significant amount to have products made. You can even legally contact manufacturers using another email ID or account to get additional samples.

- **Beware of the hidden costs** (if any) – If you feel something is too good to be true, discuss the deal in detail and if you still feel something isn't right, just walk away from it.

- **Look for the payment methods they accept** – If a manufacturer accepts PayPal or the Secure Payment System, it is a good sign for you as these are the two safest payment methods available. By using these services, you can make payment in installments, and you will not run the risk of paying for the entire amount upfront. These manufacturers might even offer dispute resolution services if one or both the parties fail to adhere to Alibaba's terms and conditions. Beware of the manufacturers who work only with the Western Union payment method as chances are high that there is a scam associated with them.

Contact Suppliers

Keep a spreadsheet of all potential suppliers that you feel are legitimate, including information such as Supplier name/link, FOB price, MOQ, Payment Terms, Gold Supplier-certified, Trade Assurance-certified and so on. This spreadsheet will help you have all the information available in one place so that you can always refer back to it.

When you are trying to contact manufacturers overseas, email is going to be your major source of communication. In most cases, particularly when you are dealing with manufacturers in non-English speaking countries, they use applications such as Google Translate to translate their email messages. To avoid misunderstandings, try to keep your email content simple, concise, spelling error free and well-formatted. This will help non-native speakers to better understand your message.

Another way to contact suppliers is to use Alibaba's instant messaging service. This instant messaging service connects with suppliers directly through their contact form, located at the bottom of the page. Clicking on Contact Supplier will take you to a different window where you can type your message and get connected.

Another means to connect with manufacturers is through Alibaba's TradeManager instant messaging service that provides you with a simple way to connect and manage your conversations.

Now that you are in touch with a reputable supplier, request a quote. Requesting a quote is quite simple on Alibaba and takes only a couple of minutes. Here are a few things you need to consider when requesting a quote:

- **Look for MOQs** – Though manufacturer might have listed a MOQ, ask again to ensure it is correct. If you feel the MOQ mentioned is high or unaffordable, provide an idea of what you can afford. Always bear in mind that MOQ is negotiable, particularly with suppliers overseas.
- **Ask for sample prices** – If you ask the manufacturer to send you a sample product so that you can check for quality, these samples might have an associated price and you should know about it before asking. Some manufacturers might charge the full retail amount to send you the sample, especially if they're getting too many requests. On the other hand, there are manufacturers who will offer a sample for free, or at least for a discounted price. So, instead of assuming things, ask any questions upfront.
- **Know the production cost and time** – More than the sample cost, it is the production cost that will make a difference in your buying decision. Ask your suppliers:
  - How much will a unit cost?

- What is the price if you order in bulk?
- Are they open to negotiating the pricing?
- What is their production time?
- How long will it take to create a product once the order is placed?

- **Ask about payment methods and terms** – While some manufacturers let you pay them in installments, some accept orders only when paid upfront. So, understand the payment method and terms of the manufacturers clearly before you make your business decision. You can also ask about payment terms for future orders.

- **Negotiate the terms and prices** – You have been communicating with the manufacturer about payment methods and terms, production costs, etc. Now it's time to negotiate the MOQs, product cost and time.

- **Ask about the logo and packing the product** – Ask the manufacturer is if they will let you customize the package they provide and whether you can apply your brand logo to the product. If you are looking for private labeling for your product, you should be able to customize and add your brand to it so that it stands out among other similar products available in the marketplace.

- **Ask about applying labels** – Ask your manufacturer how they will deal with UPC labeling of the product. Will they apply it for you, or is this something you need to handle on your end? Each product needs to have a UPC before it is shipped to Amazon, so you must know if the manufacturer is applying it for you.

If not, you will either have to get it done by a third-party agency or do it yourself. Remember that each product that goes through Amazon needs to have an FNSKU. You can ask your manufacturer to apply it for you; if not, Amazon will do it for an additional fee.

You now have all the details you need to place an order on Alibaba. Narrow down your options based on the information you have gathered such as price, MOQs, production time, payment terms and prices and the supplier's response time. If you find a deal that turns out to be too good to be true, be ready to walk away. Don't forget: there are hundreds of other options waiting for you.

If you don't hear back from a manufacturer, just remove them from your list. A supplier might not respond because:

- They're busy. A manufacturer's main job is to create products and manage tools/equipment/manpower to achieve that. Customer service or responding to disputes always takes a backseat. So, understand this well and keep sending follow-up messages. But if they take too long to respond, or do not respond at all, you need to move on and look for other options. Otherwise, you might face issues communicating with them later.
- The supplier might be on vacation. In this case, you can wait if you want to or move on to exploring the other options available.

- Your MOQ is too small. Sometimes suppliers do not show any interest if they see the MOQ is really small. They have defined MOQs for a reason and offering something that is too small can filter out your request. You can certainly propose something smaller than what they have quoted and then negotiate. Offering less, however, doesn't leave any scope for negotiations; suppliers may consider this a waste of time.

Next Steps After You Have Contacted Suppliers

Negotiation

As we have discussed in previous sections, it is fine to ask for a smaller MOQ. After all, manufacturers don't spend on buying raw materials, tools, labor, equipment each time they create products based on the effort required and size of the order. However, it will not be possible for them to produce your product for a price that is lower than the total expenses they will incur. Always consider these factors and negotiate with realistic figures. If you need a really small order, choose to go with AliExpress instead of Alibaba.

By negotiating, you are requesting that manufacturers do you a favor; you cannot, therefore, expect them to also slash their prices for you. While trying to meet your objectives, manufacturers might lower the quality of raw materials being used so that they can meet the lowered price while still making a profit. If you do not want to compromise on quality, be reasonable with the supplier and bear in mind that obtaining great quality might cost you a little extra.

There is a proper way to negotiate:

- Research as much as possible about your product including costs of raw material, production costs, production times, payment methods/ terms and shipping costs. This way you can measure the quote given by your supplier against what you already know to be true. You'll be able to judge if they have unreasonable demands on the quality, quantity and pricing.

- Be specific about details so that there is no chance of miscommunication. Be very clear about your questions and understand their responses so that neither party makes assumptions.

- If you are in touch with more than one supplier, you can perform a comparative analysis in order to make your business decision. This will enable you to determine which manufacturer is giving you a genuine quote and who is trying to take advantage of price, quality and quantity.

- Bring value to their business. You can do this by promising (and keeping your promise) that you will provide them with more clients, orders for more products and even offer them new gateways to explore new markets. This really works as the approach helps build a strong relationship between suppliers and customers.

- Be very calm and patient, but not beyond a certain limit that will affect your deadlines. Be vocal about your deadlines from the beginning and if you see your supplier will not be able to achieve the target within the defined timeframe, be ready to negotiate or move on.

- Third-party agencies and distributors mark up the product so that they can also make money. Therefore, make sure you are dealing with manufacturers directly, rather than middlemen.
- Document everything you agree on so that you can also refer to the document later in case of disagreements.
- Be professional and calm.
- Invest some time and resources if your supplier isn't taking you seriously. The main job of manufacturers is to create products and manage resources. Therefore, if they feel you aren't making inquiries with a real eye toward doing business, they will lose interest and won't waste their time on you.
- Walk away from the deal if you feel the manufacturer is trying to cheat you or is not giving you a good deal. They might come back to you later with a better price.

Commissioning a Product

If you are planning to sell something new and it doesn't already exist in the marketplace, you might need to do some research on the product before you look for someone to manufacture it for you. If your product is something similar to a product that is already on the top charts of Alibaba, you can contact suppliers who can make similar products with a modification or two. But if neither of these situations applies to your intended product, it means you are planning to sell something which is already in the marketplace (something similar), but are not able to choose which manufacturer to select. Then you can post a buying request on Alibaba. This way manufacturers will reach out to you, instead of you having to contact them.

When you have found a supplier who agrees to create your product within the defined timeline, send them the exact requirements of what you want in the product including the prototype, the wireframe, etc. If possible, send them a drawing or mockup sketch showing the exact product you need. Ensure you mention all dimensions, sizes, colors, etc. in detail; do not miss mentioning any important information as it might lead to confusion later. Give as many details as possible so that there is no room left for any issues. Be very specific about your plan and quantity so that the manufacturer is prepared for it.

Once you send all the details, along with the visual representation of how your product should look, ask for a few samples. When they send you the samples, evaluate them for quality and quantity. Conduct some tests on the product, such as a system test, drop test or whatever is appropriate to the product. The intent shouldn't be to find faults but to see if it fulfills your requirements and us durable. Send your feedback to the manufacturer and, if necessary, ask for more samples and repeat the same process until you get what you are looking for. You should not compromise on any requirements. Let them get the sample right before proceeding.

When you receive that perfect sample, place a small order and see if they can maintain a consistent quality with all products. Creating a sample might be easy, but it is important that they handle the mass production equally well. Discuss how they will handle any defective products—will they replace them or compensate you? Sometimes, particularly when the shipping cost is more, it doesn't make sense to send products back to the manufacturer. In such a case, most manufacturers either adjust the number in the next order or provide compensation.

If the small order goes smoothly and you are satisfied with what you receive, place a larger order.

What You Must Know Before Placing the Order.

While you are in the process of selecting a supplier, negotiating, receiving/ approving the samples and placing your first small order, there are certain things you must keep in mind.

- Are these products being sent to you or to the Amazon fulfillment center? If the products are being shipped to you directly, do you have enough space available to store them? If not, where will you store them?
- Have you taken into account the total costs of getting the products created? Is the number well within your budget? Has the manufacturer factored in the cost of tools and equipment required to create your products? What is the cost of one sample? What if you require more samples? Is all this within your budget? Be ready to see some additional costs and do not get carried away.

- Have you calculated your profit margins for selling this product? While calculating the profit, have you considered the cost of the product, assuming the quality remains consistent? Are you getting the right quality and quantity for the right price?

You must have a basic understanding of terms, such as intellectual property, copyrights, patents and trademarks.

- **Trademarks** – Protect the brand identity of an individual or business, such as brand names and logos
- **Copyrights** – Rights owned by a business or individual that protect the work such as content, photos, audios, videos, etc.
- **Patents** – Rights that protect ideas, such as creations, inventions, etc.

Generally, all these (copyrights, patents and trademarks) are not worthwhile as they are effective only in the country where you buy them. It's quite expensive to buy these rights and not worth it for beginners since they are just trying to develop their brand in the marketplace and likely don't have anything to protect yet. If something becomes popular and is liked by the customers on e-commerce sites such as Alibaba, others will copy that product or idea. If the manufacturers or other sellers see that something is successful, they will steal the product plan, information and pictures, and you are not protected and cannot stop it from happening. The best thing you can do to make your products and ideas stand out is to focus on your branding and marketing strategy to see how you can set your product apart from other products, whether it is in terms of price, quality or any another attribute. Beat the copycats with your innovative ideas, rather than legalities.

Establish Healthy Relationship with your Manufacturers

Your manufacturer is going to be akin to a business partner as their work will impact the success of your business. You are hugely dependent on them to give you the best possible product, and this forms the basis of your business. Therefore, always keep in mind that you need the support of your manufacturers more than anyone else. It is crucial that you establish a healthy relationship with your suppliers. Remember to:

- Always describe your requirements very clearly so that there is no room for any confusion. Be very specific about what you expect and how you want your product to be. It is always better to know things rather than assuming, so do not give them a reason to fail at meeting your expectations. They wouldn't want that either.
- Reciprocate well and on time. If you want them to respond to your queries and be available whenever you want, act the same way. After all, you get what you give. So, be there for them whenever they need something from you.
- Losing your patience can make things worse, so always be considerate and behave professionally, as a supplier might have different practices than what you follow in your country.

- Don't hesitate if you want to convey a message. It is always best to be upfront rather than facing issues later. If you do not want to be disturbed at any point, make it very clear that you are not available during that specific time. Tell them the best way to contact you, and ask them how they want to be contacted. This will make things simpler for both parties.

Shipping Information and Logistics

Shipping plays an important role in the buying process. Hence, you should know all the information and logistics about shipping before you place the order with the supplier. Remember that once shipped, products cannot be returned to the supplier, whether you like them or not. This is a no-return point. Before they ship the products to the defined destination, ensure you make two things very clear:

- Confirm and discuss their responsibilities – Reiterate their role and responsibilities in the invoice you are going to send them. Get confirmation of the cost of shipping products, agreed price of the products, the number of products that are being shipped and the expected delivery time
- Get proof of what they are sending – Before the product is shipped, ask for copies of the shipping label and photos/videos of the packaging and products.

Each supplier has their own options for shipping carriers, and you will have to select one of the options available. Each option will fall into one of these categories:

- **Sea Freight (boat)**: The carrier ships by boat. If you opt for this method, remember that although it is the cheapest means of shipping, it takes the longest.
- **Air Cargo (plane)**: The carrier ships by plane. If you opt for this method, although it is the quickest means, it will cost more. Also, not all products can be shipped by plane; for instance, some cosmetic products are considered hazardous. Make sure you research what products can and can't be shipped by air.
- **Express (train)**: The carrier ships by Express, perfect for small orders.

Once you decide which method you want for shipping, work it out with the supplier and see what they can offer.

Sourcify to Source your Products

Sourcify is the platform that helps you bring your product idea to market. Sourcify understands how daunting it is to bring a product from your imagination to the real-life market if you have never done it before. You might have a great idea, an invention that can solve a problem, a product that can help millions or an improvised alternate option for something that already exists, but you don't know how to make it real. This is where Sourcify can help you. With a mission to bring your idea to life, it introduces business owners to the right supplier, helps you with the end-to-end product development process, walks you through the process of

125

validating the legality of importing your item and allows you to make secure payments. This platform is based on a strong database that contains a comprehensive list of top-class sellers who are experts in a wide array of product manufacturing and design.

Get Started

To get started with Sourcify, join the platform, and you will be guided through each step of product development, whether you have the exact requirements of what you are looking for or just the idea. Whether you are a first-time seller or an individual/business owner who is looking to create products for better prices, Sourcify will connect you with some of the top manufacturers in the world.

The platform not only lets you source the products but also helps you sell them. And it's not just Sourcify—it's Sourcify + Shopify.

Even if you do not have any experience in coding or web designing, the platform lets you set up your online shop in a couple of minutes, list your items and start selling. You can also leverage its social marketing power to promote your product on various social handles, create followings and generate sales for your business.

Sourcify helps you evaluate the market for a product before you actually enter it. Use their dropshipping service, such as Oblero, an app that helps you import products that can be dropshipped directly into the Shopify store. Once you get an order from a customer, this product gets shipped to him/her directly. All you need to do is to keep a note of the difference in the amount you bought it for and the price you sold it for.

Canton Fair: Find the World's Best Manufacturers

Every year, hundreds of thousands of people from across the globe gather together at Canton Fair, the world's largest manufacturing tradeshow, to connect with top-class manufacturers so that they can design their business plan. Canton Fair brings together hundreds of trading companies, factories and business agents. The main reason several companies—of all sizes—come to this fair is that long-distance business relationships can break down any time, and dealing with your business partner in person can mark the beginning of a long-term relationship.

In order to attend the Canton Fair like an expert:

Do Your Homework: Research Before You Attend

If attendees do not have prior knowledge about their niche, they cannot take maximum advantage of the fair. Start researching manufacturers and potential industries online. Read about the manufacturers who are going to be present at the fair and see if you can match some of them to what you are planning to create. For example, if you are planning to sell yoga mats, search for manufacturers who offer this product. You can use the exhibitor product index to search for manufacturers.

Once you click on one of the listings from the search results, you can see details of the manufacturers, such as the name of the company/factory, the complete address, the booth number and the website link. Knowing the booth details in advance will save you time, as the fair is huge.

Socialize Before the Event: Get in touch with suppliers before you see them in person.

Try to connect with the manufacturers you are interested in working with as this gives you an advantage over others. When you look for details of manufacturers in the exhibitor product index, it gives you their email address and other contact information. Contacting them and creating a relationship before the event will give you a head start. You will feel connected when you meet them in person, and this will make the experience much better than meeting them as strangers.

Trade Show Tips:

Your main goal in visiting the fair is to find as many suppliers as possible (suppliers who can manufacture your product). With this aim in mind, doing a bit of research about who is coming to the event will help as will identifying the questions you want to ask these suppliers so that you can evaluate them and see who can do the best job for you. Some of these questions might be:

- *Do you work as an individual or do you own a trading company?* You should verify their answer by finding out the details at your end.

You can browse the Internet or check the location provided by the index in Google maps to see if a factory exists or not. You can also read blogs in forums or other threads to see what is being said.

- *In which country do you operate? Where do you send your products?* This should give you an idea of the worth of the products. Some countries are very particular about what they want and expect to receive high-quality products.

- *What kind of labels do you create? How about private labels?* This is an important question if you are an FBA private label seller. Different suppliers have different requirements if you want them to private label the products for you. Some of them can only do it if you fulfill their Minimum Order Quantity, while others have a price per unit as the criteria. If it is about MOQ, you can negotiate with them by suggesting a slightly lower number. Tell them how it will help both you and them if you can agree on the suggested number, and how you can bring them more value and business.

- *How much do you charge per unit? What are your production costs?* Price shouldn't be the top priority for you when looking for a manufacturer. Ask for the price, but don't make your business decision based on their quote and don't spend too much time discussing the pricing factor as this might send the wrong message to the supplier.

Once you have your questions answered, prepare notes. The best thing is to create an Excel sheet with the names of different manufacturers you connected with/want to connect with. Create a column for each of the questions and answers. This will make the evaluation process easier as you will have all the details for all the manufacturers in one place. Have another column where you can mark the answer, and this column needs to be filled for each manufacturer once you speak to them. This step will help you analyze which suppliers you can follow up with after the event.

It is always a good idea to reach the venue early, when there are fewer competitors, so that manufacturers/sellers can focus on you more closely.

The Post Show

Now that you have a list of the shortlisted candidates, filter out all the "negatives" and the "maybes." Follow-up with all the "Yes" candidates post-event as soon as possible, as they might not remember you if you contact them a month later. Send follow-up emails to all the "Yes" suppliers by creating a common template and tweaking it for each of them. Just use the same template and change the supplier name. Here is an example of such an email

*Dear **name of supplier or individual**,*

My name is John Petersworth, and I met you last week during the Canton Fair. I really appreciate the time you invested in our conversation, and wanted to ask few more questions about your business.

- *Can you private label your product for me?*
- *How much does your product cost per unit?*
- *What is the lead time?*

It would be really great if you could help me with this information. You can reach me at XX@YY.com.

Also, could you please provide me a few alternatives of similar products that you have so I can analyze the details with my team? Thank you for your help, and I hope to hear from you soon. It is my hope that I will be placing an order with your company.

Thanks,

John

Sending a clear, concise email like this will help your supplier understand what you want, so there is a good chance that you will hear from them.

Attending trade fairs is an important step in growing your business because it is crucial that you find the best solution and best manufacturer to create your product.

Chapter 5 – Create your Listing

In today's modern era where almost everything has been digitized, sellers with physical shops might find listing their products online challenging. Once they begin, however, listing their products becomes quite easy. With a platform like Amazon, it is even simpler. Amazon offers its sellers four different ways to list products on the website:

1. matching their products to existing ones
2. Scanning their product
3. Preparing the listing and then adding a product
4. Using the custom inventory template to list multiple products.

Matching the Product to Existing Lists

Today, there are hundreds of thousands of sellers selling their products on Amazon. To prevent these sellers from selling the same product, Amazon offers a feature known as Product Matching. When you begin to match, the platform adds quantity, shipping, price, etc. on the product page and matches the details with products available on Amazon marketplace. If the product you have entered doesn't find a match, you will be able to create the listing. However, if it finds a match, you cannot list it unless your product has unique attributes.

Scanning the Product

If you have the Amazon Seller App, you can list your product by simply scanning the barcode of your product. As these barcodes are unique, the scanner uniquely identifies the product.

Preparing Your Listing and Add the Product

If you have all the product information, you can list your product using another option—by preparing the listing. Just click on the Prepare Your Listings tab and then click on Add a Product. It will then ask for product details, categories, etc. to add your product.

Using Custom Inventory Template to List Multiple Products

Using the Inventory tab, you can add a product to the marketplace. This option lets you list multiple products at once. Include all the product details and start publishing.

Matching the Product to the Existing List

1. **Search** for the product you want to list on Amazon. Once you find a match, click on Sell Yours Here. Next, it will ask you for other details, so fill in the information needed and proceed.

2. **Describe the condition** of your item. Amazon gives you a list of options to choose from to describe the condition of your listing based on what you are trying to sell. In this field, you can choose the option from the drop-down menu and add comments, if any. For our favorite example of a yoga mat, you can choose the condition as Good and mention "Brand new with intact cover." Take pains to describe your item

correctly. If there are any defects, this is the place to declare them. Your buyers respect honesty and accuracy and will provide good feedback if you show that in your comments.

3. **Rate your listing**. There are four major categories you can sell your products under— New, Collectible, Used and Refurbished. Grade your items so that your customers will be satisfied when they receive their items. Amazon provides various categories:

   o New: Your product is brand new, unopened and the customer will receive it in its original packing, with the original warranty (if any). Any warranty should be mentioned very clearly on the product.

   o Like New: The product looks like new, with no signs of wear. The original plastic packaging might be missing, but the original packing is otherwise intact with all instructions included, if any.

   o Very Good: The product is well-preserved but has undergone limited use. Although undamaged, it might have some signs of wear. The condition of the product is excellent and undamaged, complete and unmarked. There is no issue with the item's functionality.

   o Good: The product has been used for some time and the wear caused is due to the consistent use. Although it is in good condition, it might be marked and have prominent signs of wear. Functionality-wise, there are no issues with the product.

- o Refurbished: The product was inspected and repaired to its original specifications. Although the original packing might not be included, the warranty, as per the repairs, should be included and applied.
- o Acceptable: The product is worn, but works properly. There are signs of wear that includes dents, scratches and various aesthetic issues. The product might be marked.
- o Unacceptable: The product is worn out and doesn't work properly. Due to this, it cannot be sold on Amazon because items that are damaged or need service are not acceptable.

4. **Set your Selling Price**. Now that you have categorized and rated your product, set the selling price accordingly, bearing its condition in mind.

Your listing can be priced from 1 cent up to $2500 but to maximize your profits, set the price close to the cost listed by your competitors. It doesn't have to be too low, as you will lose your profits, but at the same time, if you set it too high, your sales might be impacted. Do not forget about the costs for handling, packaging and shipping.

5. **Set other options** including the shipping location. In order to set the shipping location, enter the zip code of the area where it needs to be shipped from. This will give the buyer an idea of the distance. You also need to enter if the item has to be shipped internationally. This can

attract more customers, but you will need to set the price accordingly. In case the product is oversized, it might exceed the shipping credit, and hence the selling price should be increased if it is to be shipped internationally.

Certain items are marked as Collectibles on Amazon. These are special edition items that can be sold at a premium price. Sellers are free to set the price for these items as long as they adhere to the guidelines provided by Amazon. The general pricing rule is that products that are priced more than $10 or above the manufacturer's list price (whichever is greater), can be tagged as Collectibles. Your item on Amazon should be priced around or below the price for the product on other sites. Suppose you are selling a yoga mat at $20 on eBay. Amazon expects you to sell it for $20 or a lower price, including all costs.

6. **Set the SKU and quantity**. An SKU, or Stock Keeping Unit, is used to identify an item being sold. Your inventory can be managed using SKU IDs as you assign these unique IDs to your items. For an item to be listed and sold on Amazon, it must have an SKU. If you have a seller's account on Amazon, it will generate an SKU for your item. If you have a Professional account, you can specify what SKU you want or let Amazon fill in the SKU for your item. If you are selling multiples of the same item, insert the number of items in the Quantity field of the listing form. But keep in mind, everything about

these copies of items should be exactly same, including the condition. Otherwise, create different listings for each of these copies, keeping the quantity as 1. Also, in each category, you can add a maximum of five identical items.

7. **Proceed to Payments**. Amazon handles all payments for any sale that happens on their platform. It doesn't allow any third-party payment systems like PayPal. All buyers have to pay for their orders using Amazon's payment system and Amazon then collects and transfers funds to the sellers through this system. This safeguards buyers as well as sellers because if there are any disputes, they will be handled by Amazon only.

8. **Identify your products** on Amazon using unique identifiers such as Universal Product Codes (UPC) or European Article Numbers (EAN). These codes uniquely identify what you are selling and even help you sell them faster. Items can also be identified using an Amazon Standard Identification Number (ASIN), which is created when there is no standard ISBN or UPC assigned to an item. This ASIN can be found under Product Details, or you can look for the identifier in the browser address bar.

We have discussed private labeling, where you get the product created and label it with your own brand. Let's create a listing for your brand product on Amazon. Although each product is unique and might need some additional steps to get listed, here is the basic step-by-step process to list a product on Amazon using the

Inventory method. By the end of this chapter, you should be able to create your listing.

1. **Log in** to your Seller account and click on the Add a Product tab, which appears under the Inventory tab. Although this is not the only way of adding a product, it's the easiest of all and perfect for beginners.

2. **Choose** one of the three methods that appear when you click on the Add a Product option.

   ➤ The first option is to add a product that already exists on Amazon by searching for its name or ID.

   ➤ The second option is to add the new product by clicking on Create a New Product Listing below the search bar. This is used when you need to upload a brand-new product on Amazon, one that is not currently being sold.

   ➤ The last option is to bulk upload the products. This is used when you want to list more than one product all at once. For now, let's see how to add a new product, per option two.

3. **Click on Create a New Product Listing** and you will be asked to enter the category your product belongs to. You can find the category either by using the search option of the platform or by looking through various categories available. If you go with the Search option, just type in the product name in the search bar and click on Find Category. Amazon will give you a list of options to choose for categories.

4. **From the categories listed**, choose the one that best fits your product.
5. **Fill in all the required information** needed to list your product. You will see that the information needed is divided under 7 different headings:
    o Vital Info
    o Variations
    o Offer
    o Images
    o Description
    o Keywords and
    o More Details.

Let us look at each of these categories.
- **Vital info** – This heading is comprised of:
    o Product Name
    o Manufacturer
    o Brand Name
    o Manufacture's Part Name
    o Package Quantity
    o Material Type
    o Color/Color Map
    o Shape
    o Lens Color
    o Size
    o Hand Orientation and Tension Supported
    o GTIN Exemption Reason
    o Related Product ID Type and Product ID
    o Item Display Dimensions and Weight
    o Weight Supported and Display Maximum Weight Recommendations
    o Shaft Length and

o   Product ID.

The Product Name – the title that is visible to everyone who sees your listing. It's the first thing that catches your customer's attention, so use a catchy and interesting product name by adding as many keywords and attributes of the product as possible. For example, instead of naming your product "Yoga Mat," name it "Extra Flexible Waterproof Yoga Mat." Note: 250 characters is the maximum for the title. So optimize the title as best you can.

Manufacturer and Brand Name – mention your own brand name for both fields if you are private labeling the product.

Manufacturer's Part Name – not required unless you are listing a product that's a replacement part of another existing product.

Package Quantity – the number of products you are selling.

Material Type – offers you a list of materials to choose from. Click on the box and you will see the options. Select the one that is appropriate for your product.

Color field – refers to the color of your product and Color Map is the base color that is associated with your product. For now, you can leave the Color Map field as blank.

Shape – refers to the shape of your product. If you feel it is not applicable, leave it blank.

Lens Color – denotes the color of the lens in the product. Leave it blank unless the product comprises colored lenses.

For Size – enter the dimensions of your product correctly. You can enter a numeric value of the text version.

For Hand Orientation – mention this if the item is built for lefties or righties. Leave it blank if you feel it's not applicable to your product.

Tension Supported – the amount of tension that can be borne by the product.

GTIN Exemption Reason – stands for the reason you get an exemption from having a unique identifier for your item. Almost all the products are required to have a Global Trade Identifier Number (GTIN) associated with them, which is similar to a UPC or ISBN. But some products are exempted from this if they belong to certain specified categories. Amazon has created a list of these categories that you can refer to, to understand whether your product can be exempted.

For Related Product ID Type and Related Product ID – enter the type and product ID of the related product. If your product is not related to anything, do not fill in these fields

Item Display Dimensions and Weight – will have the length, width and weight of the product.

Weight Supported – the given weight capacity of the item. If your item is not designed to support any weight, leave it blank.

Display Maximum Weight Recommendation – the recommended value of displayed weight. Again, if your product doesn't support any weight, do not fill in this field.

Shaft Length – the length of the shaft of your product.

Product Id – the unique product ID (UPC, GCID or EAN). As mentioned previously, any product that has to be listed on Amazon must have a unique Product ID, which distinguishes it from other products listed. If you are private labeling, you need to buy your own Product ID for the newly created product but if you are not, check with the supplier to see if he has the information.

- **Variations** – displays information about the variations available for your product, for example—a variety of sizes or colors, width, loft or any other attributes. From the drop-down menu, choose the type of variation available that matches your product. Once you select the type of variation, there are more fields that appear to give clarification for your listing. So just select the type of variation you want based on your product and click on Add Variations. Add all the pertinent information for each variation.

- **Offer** – contains information about your listing, such as Import Designation, Country of Publication, Seller Warranty Description, etc. Let us look at each of these fields.

  - Import Designation – gives the import information about your product. If your product is made in the US from materials imported from other places, state "Made in the USA and Imported." If your product is made in the USA from USA material, state "Made in the USA."

- Country of Publication – provides details about the country where your product is published. If your product is not published yet, skip this.
- Seller Warranty Description – needs to be filled in if you offer any sort of guarantee or warranty with your product. For example, you can mention, "If you find any flaws with the product, I offer you a full money-back guarantee."
- Release Date – should have the first date that you can deliver your order. Fill this in only if you want your customers to know when you are planning to release your product.
- The Country as Labeled – should have the name of the country where the product was created (if not the USA) and if the label has the name of the country of origin.
- Is Gift Wrap Available & Offering Can be Gift Messaged – should be filled in if you are not using Amazon's FBA service and want to offer a gift wrapping and messaging service for your product.
- Tax Code – should be entered if you are using Amazon tax collection for your product.
- Fulfillment Latency – the time between when you get the order for your product

and when you ship it to the customer. If you are not using FBA, mention the time it will take for you to ship the product from the day the order is placed.

- o Restock Date – the date that you wish to have the stock replenished.
- o Legal Disclaimer – should be entered if you have any guidelines for your customers. If you are not sure about the exact words, consult your supplier.
- o Start Selling Date – when you will start selling your product on Amazon.
- o Signed By – should have the name of the individual who signed your product.
- o Fulfillment Channel – where you need to mention if you want your orders to be Fulfilled by Amazon or will fulfill them on your own. Keep in mind the pros and cons of both the options before you make your choice.

- **Images** – this is where you need to upload the images of your product. Do not forget to adhere to the guidelines provided by Amazon while selecting images that you want to be displayed.
- **Description** – This tab has just two attributes that you need to take care of: Key Product Features and Product Description.
  - ➤ Key Product Features field should have the key attributes of your product that will appear as bullet points at the top of your listing. According to experts, Amazon evaluates your listings and ranks

them based on the keywords you choose to use in these bullet points. Always remember to use as many keywords as you can for this field.

Although Amazon claims to accept only 100 characters for this field, they do not truncate the sentence even if it has more than the defined limit. Experts recommend making the best use of the space by using as many keywords as you can.

> Product Description – This field offers you another opportunity to promote your products and get more sales. Use it to talk about the benefits your product can bring to your customers—why they should buy it? Do not just talk about various features of your product; explain the uses and how your product can help them solve their problems. For this field, Amazon allows 2000 characters.

- **Keywords** – The Keyword tab is the most important feature of the Amazon listing. Although customers may not pay attention to what you enter in this tab, Amazon uses these keywords to display results whenever anyone searches for your product.
  > Search Terms – should be filled in with as many keywords as possible, and note that these keywords should be unique and

related to your product. They should not be separated using a comma. You shouldn't repeat keywords, so if you have used a keyword in the product title or the description, do not mention it again here.

➤ Platinum Keywords – should only be filled in if you are a platinum seller on Amazon. Most sellers are not Platinum sellers, so you most likely do not need to worry about this.

➤ Subject Matter – should have the information about your product's subject (what it is about.) You can select a relevant option from the drop-down menu provided.

➤ Other Attributes – should be filled in if you have additional attributes about your product that you need to mention. Again, this is a drop-down field, so choose whatever you feel is relevant.

➤ Intended Use – state what events, purposes or activities your product can be used for. Pick the relevant options from the drop-down menu.

➤ Target Audience – indicates data about who you are trying to target. Again, choose the relevant options from the drop-down.

• **More Details** – customized based on your product and the category it belongs to. Once you enter the product and product category, see what fields appear in this tab and complete them appropriately.

Once you have filled in the relevant information in all the tabs, click on Save and finish the job. If the tab grays out and doesn't proceed, it means you have missed something that was mandatory. Go back to the tabs and see if you missed entering some essential piece of information.

You have completed all the steps to list your product on Amazon and it's official now. You will still need to figure out the shipping options if you have opted for FBA service.

How to Improve Your Listing

Being a seller on Amazon is not enough; it is important to be on the top charts of your potential customers to grow your numbers. To achieve this, sellers are always looking for various options to optimize their listings, particularly by studying their competition. If someone is doing business on Amazon in the same niche as you and has an optimized listing as well as an awesome ranking, the seller is your competition. Listings can be optimized by:

o   Using better quality images
o   Using titles that are keyword optimized
o   Getting more customer reviews
o   Finding a pricing sweet spot
o   Using bullets and descriptions that sell

Just making these changes is not enough. You need to test your listing performance after making each of these changes so that you know if it made any difference. For example, if you added a few more keywords to the title, you need to test whether it helped improve your sales. However, don't test right after making the change. Give it some time to take effect and then test.

Study what your competitors are up to on a regular basis. If they are already doing great in the niche, you should watch how and what they are doing. See what they are doing well. Learn from them, as they are the so-called experts in your niche. Knowing what they do should help you to advance your business. But before you start studying your competition, ensure you are studying the right competitor. Keep the following in mind:

- o The brand you are planning to study might be at the top spot, but look carefully at who it is. Is the brand a bigtime, nationwide selling business? If yes, you might not want to consider it, as nationally well-known sellers might be breaking the rules of listing on Amazon. They must be popular due to their brand recognition, which you do not have yet.
- o It might be possible that the brand you are planning to study is new to Amazon, just like you, and is trying out various things to get on the first page of search results. You can tell if this is the case by checking reviews and rankings. If the seller has only a few reviews on this product, and a poor ranking, he might be a newcomer to the market. If so, drop that one and move on, as studying that brand wouldn't teach you anything.

o If you are confused about which brand and which competitor to study, go with the one which has high ratings, isn't a nationwide seller and is a brand that doesn't have multiple listings on Amazon. Although all the competitors will give you some good information, if you go by these preferences, you will learn the most from your market analysis.

To start the process of studying the competition, make note of the following:

1. *How many reviews does the competitor have?* Make sure you check the reviews that are applicable to your listing.
2. *What does their product lack?* Look for your competitor's weaknesses. This can be done by reading the negative reviews, overlooking the ones that are trivial. Look to see if there is something that more than one person has commented on. If the listing really lacks something, its weakness can be your strength. Try to solve the problems of those unhappy customers by giving them what they are looking for.
3. *What are their strengths?* Check the positive reviews in your competition's listing. Read the reviews to see what people like best about the product. Can you incorporate something similar in your product? By making simple and easy tweaks to your listing, you can make it more competitive.
4. *What are the keywords that your competition has used?* Look for the product description,

product heading, bullet points of the competitor's listing and check what keywords they have used. Since the seller is someone who is doing really well in the marketplace, he or she must have done a lot of research on the keywords. Next, see if these keywords can be used for your listing. However, you cannot use them in your listing as-is. You will have to tweak them as per your listing and play around with the wording a bit to make it unique.

How to Manage your Listings

You have listed your products and optimized the listings. Each time you list an item, you've received an email confirmation from Amazon. And each time the status of your listing has changed, you've also received an email message. If you do not want to look at these emails, just check your listings by looking for them in your seller's account a few minutes after the submission. Just checking them is not enough, however; you need to properly manage them against your competitors, ensuring your listings are accurate and up-to-date. To do this:

1. Click on View your Current Inventory from your seller account to see your Open Listings in the marketplace.
2. Change the price or quantity of any item by clicking on Edit. If you need to change the condition from Good to Unacceptable, you cannot edit your listing; you will have to relist it again.

3. Submit your listing once all the changes are made. If you want to edit something again, click on Edit.

Apart from editing, you can click Close Listing at any point in time before any buyer places an order. If that becomes necessary, close the listing and save changes.

If you want to search any listing, you can do it using various attributes, sorted by various parameters, including price, product name, price, SKU and so on. To change the way your listing is displayed, you can Set your Preferences from the Open Listings page.

The most important attribute is price. As discussed previously, setting the price for your item once is not enough. You should monitor your competition and reprice your listing from time to time, to stay competitive. If you are not up-to-date, you will either lose on your profit margins or sales.

If you go to the Open Listing page, you will see the Low Price feature that can help you compare the price of your listing with prices of similar items being sold by competitors. Look at the comparative values and update your listing accordingly. This feature of Low Price offers you three options:

1. You can compare your listing with all other listings of the same product on Amazon, not considering the condition.
2. You can compare your listing with other listings of the same product on Amazon that are in the same condition as your product (New, Used, Collectible, Refurbished).

3. You can compare your listing with other listings in the same sub-condition (Good, Very Good, New, etc.)

Repricing your Listings

Repricing depends on various parameters and on the type of product you are selling, your business strategy and so on. Nobody wants to sell an item for a lower price, but sometimes it becomes important to make a sale. In Amazon's marketplace, you have to always compete to offer the best price as normally buyers will look at only two or three prices. Once you win the confidence of your buyers, you will not have to compete solely on the basis of price. You will be considered by the buyers on the basis of reviews you have earned. On the other hand, if you keep prices too low, you might not even appear on the top listings. Some sellers always maintain low prices for their listings in order to appear on the top. But it's not necessary to always cut prices to be at the top; you just have to match the price. You can use automated tools (previously discussed) to help you price your items better, especially for items below $10 or $20.

How you price your items also depends on the type of product. You might have a different pricing strategy for different parts of your inventory. If you are selling New items, you can expect them to make a specific profit margin. If you are selling unique items like used CDs, books, etc. you can be more aggressive about the price.

Relisting the Items

Regular Amazon account listings expire in 60 days. After that, the items need to be relisted again using the manual method from the Open Listings page. But for Professional account holders, the listing remains valid until an item is sold out.

Chapter 6 – Product Launch

When you launch your product, you should have two goals in mind: getting sales and reviews. Consider these two as something that will give you the momentum you need to grow your business. To get ranked in the top charts of most popular search engines, you and your products need to get noticed by potential customers.

People look for products on Amazon by typing in keywords/product names in the search bar. If they find something interesting, they click through and find more details about it. On the basis of these details, they make their purchase decision. So, your ultimate goal should be to make your listing appear in the search results when someone types in keywords related to the product you are selling on Amazon. For instance, if you are selling power yoga mats, if someone types in power yoga, your product listing should appear in the top list of the search results. Some of the other keywords you might want to use in your listing to get noticed might be durable yoga mat, soft yoga mat, etc.

When you are ranked in the search results pages, your customers will be able to discover you and purchase your product. But when a new product is listed, like yours, it probably goes on page 20 or 25, where it never gets noticed by customers. Thus, the only way to be seen is to appear on the first page, which is where most sales happen. This is the reason sales are one of the key things to get noticed. Once you are visible and gain notice, then reviews start playing a role.

Get More and More Reviews

Shoppers often look at the reviews of a product or service before making their purchase decisions. Therefore, it is important for you to accrue sales and reviews on your listing. One effective strategy to start making sales is offering your customers a giveaway promotion. Promotions are really good at driving sales. As a giveaway promotion to get sales started, you can offer buyers at least a 50 percent discount on your listing. You can list these promotions on deal websites such as Jump Send, where people normally go to look for discounted products. If you research these deal sites, you will see that there are steep discounts offered on products—anywhere from 50 per cent to even 90 percent off on certain items. By offering steep discounts, the sellers guarantee good sales— definitely a lot more than by giving away the product at its original price. These discounts might mean you are likely to lose money on your product, but when you start a business you need these promotions to drive initial sales and get your listing launched effectively and ranked on the top pages.

Using Amazon's Sponsored Products – PPC Program

Sponsored Products, a PPC program that exists within Amazon and uses keywords, is a platform which is an effective traffic driving mechanism. You can either look for the keywords or let the platform find them for you using its own mechanism. Although this type of targeting is similar to various other platforms such as Adwords, Amazon's strategy is quite different. With this, you also pay an amount whenever someone clicks on your ad. That's because this click drives traffic to your site or listing by taking the user directly to your listing, where the buyer can make the purchase. Thus, the detail page becomes a powerful direct link to the ad.

Sponsored Products impact the overall market value of a seller by providing acceleration to the newer and low-exposure products. Based on your goals, Amazon can help you build campaigns to launch your product or feature an existing product. This can be done in two ways—Automatic, which targets ads to a relevant audience based on product information, and Manual where sellers can manually set keyword options for the campaign.

Now, let's look at how to offer promotions. Log into your seller account and navigate to Manage Product Selection if you have not set up any promotion before. Next, navigate to Create Product Selection. This is where you will decide the products to which you want to apply the promotion. Select the ASIN List for all the products that you wish to be affected by the promotion and the create-product selection. You can use any name you want for the product selection as this is for Internet purposes only. Add in all the ASINs that you want to be included in the promotion, submit the list and see that the product selection has been created successfully.

1. **Navigate to Create a Promotion** (Percentage Off). Normally what you see as a default is the least number of items that are recommended for the promotion. But you can choose the amount in dollars and even the quantity of items that the buyer purchases to get this promotion. What you

select here will determine how the promotion will be triggered. For instance, when you click on the purchased items it will show you all the product selections. Now select the product selection you have created for the promotion and your customers will get a percentage off on this product selection. This is where you can select the amount of discount you want to offer to your customers who purchase your product. For example, if you enter 20 percent in this field, all the selected items will be discounted by 20 percent.

2. **Perform Scheduling.** While creating promotions, keep in mind that a promotion on Amazon needs to start at least four hours in the future. You can expect the promotion to be active anytime after that. Another important thing is to set your end date—when you want your promotion to end. Setting the date and time when you want your promotion to end on Amazon helps in protecting your inventory. By default, if there is no limit applied, a customer can purchase any number of your products. To stop this from happening, Amazon lets sellers set a limit on the number of items a buyer can purchase. This means customers can only buy up to the quantity you have set. But this limitation is applicable only until the promotion end date. So ensure the promotion ends at the same time or before that date.

Another field that you need to populate is Internal Description. You can add anything, as this is for internal use only.

3. The code you have provided be claimed once (Single-use), Multiple times (Group) or None. It is recommended that you select Single-use. If "One Redemption Per Customer" is checked, this means the customer can use the redemption code only once. Another field in this step is Claim Code, which should be set to exclusive. This means that the provided promotion code cannot be combined with any other code or offer.

Uncheck the box that asks if you want your promotion to appear as public so that not everyone can see and use your promotion code. Once this is done, navigate to Review. Ensure you check all the details thoroughly and then click on Submit. This successfully creates your promotion.

4. Create coupon codes. Browse through View or Modify on the promotion tab and manage the codes. You can use whatever codes you want for this. Set these codes and click on Create. Once the codes are created, you can download them as a zip file. When you open this zip file, you will see all the codes you have created. Simply copy them and paste them into your discount website. Now you are all set to go.

Pay-Per-Click on Amazon (Sponsored Ads)

Amazon offers its users a platform for advertising their listings, known as the Pay-Per-Click platform or PPC. This is where your listing will appear above others. To set it up, the most important thing is to select the keywords that you would like to appear and the amount you can pay to make these keywords appear. For example, if your listing is currently displayed on page 22; you can make it appear on page 1 by paying a certain amount. This way it will get good exposure in the marketplace under the keywords you have selected. At first, when you start out, you will have two types of options to consider to advertise your listing: automatic campaigns and automated email campaigns.

Automatic Campaigns

To set up the automatic campaign:

- Log into your Seller Account on Amazon and go to the Advertising Campaign Manager.
- Click on Create Campaign. It will ask you to provide a campaign name and the amount you want as your daily budget. Let's say you are okay to spend $10 a day for campaigning your product. Enter these fields and click on Continue. You can then select the product that you want to advertise and give it a name.
- Scroll down and select a default bid for this product. You can enter anything here, even $1. This doesn't mean you will spend $1 each time someone clicks on your listing; it means that this is the maximum amount you can afford to pay. If your competitor bids 50 cents, you can bid just 60 cents. Bear in mind that $1 is a large amount if you are just starting out with your business, so try to keep it at 40 cents or 60 cents. Later you can edit the amount.
  After a couple of days, if you feel you are not getting many views or impressions, you can

increase the default bid because the reason why people are not clicking could be the low bid amount and others might be bidding higher. This might be the reason your ad isn't showing up, so it is good to up the amount a bit.

- Select the bid value and click Save to finish the setting. This will start the automatic campaign. When you start, Automatic campaigns are recommended for a number of reasons including the fact that they are really simple and quick to set up.

Once you set up the campaign, it will start to collect data for you. When you start, you won't really know what the effective keywords are for your products. Amazon helps you by displaying the keywords it feels are most relevant to your listing. After running the automatic campaign for six to seven days, you can download a report that gives you complete information on what keywords Amazon is displaying for you. Using this information, you can find the best-performing keywords for your product and then create a manual campaign by keying in these words.

With a manual campaign, you have some control over the budget for your listing. In these campaigns, you have an option to add up to 1000 keywords, and you can continue to refine the keywords based on how they perform. When you see a keyword giving you the best conversion rate, the job is done. Use this keyword and increase your bids. When the keywords are getting too many clicks but a low conversion rate, reduce the bids.

Another reason why you might want to consider PPC is its large audience base. Amazon is a platform where people go to buy various products and services. Many of these customers are not at the top of the marketing funnel (Awareness, Consideration, Purchase, Retention); they just know what they need to purchase and are looking for someone who can offer them a product that is ready to be bought. Therefore, with Amazon, you can get a good number of impressions and return on investment. If you are worried about reaching an audience outside the Amazon circle, don't be. Amazon has a huge audience base, and by creating campaigns on this platform, you can build awareness of your listing as well as exposure.

Return on Investment is another compelling reason why you might want to run these automatic campaigns. When you carefully plan and create campaigns, you build an organic ranking for your listing, which eventually helps sales increase.

Automated Email Campaigns

Besides the automatic campaigns, Amazon offers you automated email campaigns that send follow-up emails to potential customers. It is a great advertising tool that also encourages your customers to leave reviews apart from getting sales. You can achieve both the targets— getting more sales and reviews. While not each customer is going to write a review for your product, some of them will and the possibility of this increases by using the automatic email campaigns.

You can use different types of templates to send follow-up emails to customers. These can be either blank or pre-made, based on what you want to include. One of the great things about the email templates is their auto-fill tags. These tags automatically download the required information from the order form such as buyer's name, order link for this buyer, etc. This makes your job really simple as you can just edit minor things and send the email. You can even add an attachment to the email, such as an eBook or a PDF document. Essentially, you have various options to choose from in order to send emails to your potential customers.

Manual Campaigns

You can build your manual campaigns by adding keywords to the SKU that you want to bid. You can identify the top keywords by evaluating product sales, the highest number of clicks, orders, etc. If the selected keywords do not work due to shifts in the market or other strange trends, you can continue the keyword harvesting process to look for more keywords. Sometimes some of the keywords do not get many impressions although they are relevant to your listing. This is because Amazon considers many attributes when running Sponsored Ads; they look at reviews, your sales history, velocity and so on. This is because they want to provide the best experience to their customers.

There are various ways to optimize your PPC campaigns for maximum Return on Investment.

First, set up your top goals for what you really expect from these PPC campaigns. You can aim to find new keywords to

- make your campaigns more effective cut wasted expenditure or
- enhance the profitable conversions.

Before we look at ways to attain these goals, let's look at some of the features of this kind of marketing that sellers are often not sure about. One of these features is the *Match Types*. When researching keywords for your campaign, you can use three match types:

- Broad Match type
- Phrase Match type and
- Exact type.

These match types help you understand the kind of audience you have.

Broad Match type: This type of keyword allows the platform to show your ad on a broad basis to your target audience. This means that the keywords you have highlighted will be matched to searched keywords that not just match your keywords but are also related. These can include misspellings, synonyms and variations of the selected keywords. How does this help? Certainly, if you advertise in a broad way, you will be able to target a larger set of consumers. However, if you have a larger audience from broader matches, you are likely to pay for more clicks from people who might not be interested in your listing.

Hence, the conversion rate on the broader match words might not be great as compared to the précised search rate. Someone looking for a similar product might click on your product but immediately move to another listing to buy it as they might find a closer match with that listing. This way you might be able to drive traffic to your listing, but this traffic might not be considered qualified. One plus of this type of search is that it will give you data on what buyers are searching for in the marketplace so you can use broad match type search to analyze the market and later adjust the keywords to match the exact search words.

Phrase Match type: Phrase Match type search lets you narrow your search results based on exact phrases. The most important feature of this kind of match is that it lets you control word order. This match will not show search items that have terms between the words in your select phrase, but it will include search terms that have unwanted words before or after the keyword phrase, along with variations of the selected phrase. These variations can include misspellings, acronyms, stemming, plurals, singulars and abbreviations of the keyword.

Using Phrase Match type, you can eliminate all customers who are not interested in your product as your ad will not appear for search terms that have words in between your phrase. Therefore, you are narrowing the field of your potential customers. This type of match is great when you want to analyze the market for specific phrases your potential customers are looking for. Using this data, you can target the customers who are looking for products similar to yours.

Exact Match type: Exact Match is capable of narrowing the field of your target customers even more (as compared to Broad match and Phrase Match) as it asks for the Exact Match, which is as specific in terms of looking for qualified traffic to your listing. Using an Exact Match, you can narrow the options for your target audience who are searching for exclusive keywords. As with phrase match, this match type will filter even the close variations of your keywords but not the phrases that have words before or after your keyword. It will not even include synonyms for the select keywords. Therefore, this type of match reduces the number of potential customers who can see your ad, so that those who see your ad are more likely to click through. The challenge is to find the exact keywords, and the task is time-consuming. The time invested is worth it because once you are able to figure those keywords out, you can efficiently drive traffic to your site or listing.

The most effective way to search for keywords is to analyze data derived from Broad Match. By analyzing those results, you can get an idea of the search terms your potential customers are looking for. Using this information, you can uncover the exact keywords for the Exact Match type and create a better conversion rate for your listing.

Each search type comes with its own set of pros and cons. While Broad Match gives you filtered results, Phrase Match will give you matches that are closer to your keyword. As you move from one type to another, you eliminate some of the options, narrowing the result to find the Exact Match for your keyword. The ultimate goal is to find the best choice for your keyword that drives a great conversion rate along with the clicks. If you are just starting with your listing, always run a Broad Match type first to analyze what your customers are looking for. Once you have this data, you can try Phrase Match types and Exact Match types to further narrow your options to find the keyword that can get you the highest click-through rate.

Next, familiarize yourself with Search Term Reports. If you log onto your Seller Account and look under Advertising Reports, you will see how useful these can be in optimizing your results. You can download the reports and keep them handy either in a PDF or Excel format. Become familiar with this report so that you can do deep research, analyze the marketplace based on various filters and see which keywords are doing well and will get you great results in terms of sales and reviews.

Let us return to the three goals we discussed earlier: cutting down on wasted spending, looking for keywords to make your campaigns more effective and enhancing profitable conversions.

Cutting Down on Wasted Spending

We can always cut down on excess expenditure by using certain strategies, such as deleting keywords that are not helping us, enhancing the words' relevancy and quality of traffic to the listing and by adjusting bids.

Looking for New Keywords

Having just a strategy is not enough; you should see some good numbers also. To make your campaign effective, you should know how to use the search term reports to find new keywords that can perform and convert well. One of the best ways to do this is to filter results based on the sales produced so that you can find keywords that already have some sales associated with them. You can then use this data to find exact keywords through the means of an Exact Match campaign.

Enhancing the Profitable Conversions

According to experts, Amazon prefers Exact Match over the other two match types. For instance, if you are eyeing a keyword in Phrase Match and another seller is looking at the same keyword as an Exact Match, Amazon will prefer the ad for the Exact Match. This might be because Exact Match allows more controlled bidding and allows you to identify the keywords that make a difference in your business by converting well.

Utilize the Power of Lightning Deals

Promotional deals that are available to users on Amazon for a limited time are known as Lightning Deals. If you are looking to reduce your inventory quickly and simply, include your product in the deal to see your sales increasing. These Lightning Deals can be found within the Gold Box Deals. If you have a Professional seller account, you can add your products to the Lightning Deals by checking your Lightning Deals dashboard. When determining eligibility, Amazon considers various criteria, such as product reviews, the category of the product, etc.

Product reviews: The platform only uses good quality products to feature in their promotional Lightning Deals. To be chosen for these deals, a product must have at least a three-star rating (subject to change based on the various attributes). But an important thing to keep in mind is the more reviews you have on your listing, the less influence a negative rating will have on your profile. Thus, it clearly is important to try to get as many reviews as possible.

Product category: Certain products are considered offensive or inappropriate and are not considered to be eligible for Lightning Deals. Some of these products include alcohol, adult products, medical devices and so on.

Fulfillment method: For an item to be listed in the Lightning Deal, it must be Prime eligible, either through Merchant-Fulfilled Prime or via Fulfillment by Amazon.

Variations: If there are variations of your product, Amazon might specify that some of them be included in the Lightning Deal. This list of products is refreshed once a week.

If your product is listed in the dashboard as deal eligible, you can present it for the deal in either of two ways:

- Navigate to the Create tab of the Deal Dashboard and then click on the product you want to add. Edit the settings to set the cost, quantity, variations and schedule.
- Navigate to See all Recommendations, and this will take you all the way through the creation process, helping you with prompts at each step.

Pay attention to details, such as price, quantity, variation, etc.

Price: Amazon considers deals that can offer attractive discounts (at least 20 percent) to customers.

Quantity: You can set the quantity of products you want to add to the deal. Amazon provides seven days before the deal is scheduled to run if the inventory you have has a large enough quantity of items. If not, Amazon has the authority to cancel your deal.

Variation: If you have variations of your product, Amazon might specify 'x' percentage of those variations be included in the deal. It recommends that sellers include as many variations in their Lightning Deals as possible as this reduces the odds of the deals being rejected.

Frequency: Amazon aims to keep its deals fresh and varied for the benefit of its customers. Hence, it doesn't allow sellers to run a deal on the same product (ASIN) for more than seven days.

Schedule: Although you cannot select the exact time or day when the deal should run, you can mention the week. In case the created deal is selected by Amazon, it will contact you about the exact schedule when the deal is to run.

Use the Lightning Deal Dashboard to stay updated on the status of the deal you just created. Amazon uses different statuses to help you keep track of your Lightning Deal.

Draft: This status means the deal is still not complete, and you have made at least one mistake in setting it up on the dashboard. If you see the status of Draft, go back to your deal and correct/complete the field values as necessary until the issue is resolved. Once done, you can submit the edited deal again.

Under Review: This status means the deal has been set up and is waiting for approval by Amazon. Amazon sometimes immediately approves or rejects deals, but in certain cases, it can take up to 15 minutes to review the deal. Therefore, if you see the status of your Lightning Deal as Under Review, check again after a couple of minutes.

Pending: This status means that your Lightning Deal has been cleared and you will hear from Amazon within a week about the exact time of the day for the schedule of the run.

Needs Edits: This status indicates your deal has not passed Amazon's checks and that there are highlighted areas that need to be edited. Make the necessary edits and then re-submit the edited deal for approval.

Upcoming or Approved: This status means that the deal has been approved and scheduled.

Suppressed: This status means that your deal has not cleared the eligibility criteria and has been suppressed by Amazon. The reason might be that the discount you have set doesn't appeal, or you might have included percentages of the variations that are too high. It is even possible that your rating has fallen below the minimum requirement (three-star rating). Check all these points to see what has happened. To know the exact reason for the rejection, you can go to the information button next to the ASIN. If you want your deal approved, make appropriate changes to the quantity, price, or inventory and at least 25 hours before the schedule.

You can choose to withdraw your Lightning Deal at any time if the deal is yet to start or has already started. But if you choose to cancel your deal less than 25 hours prior to the scheduled time of the deal, you will have to pay a fine. Last-minute cancellations increase the chances that you can be blacklisted from submitting Lightning Deals in the future. It is important that you check all the details beforehand and regularly check the status once you submit the deal. This will give you enough time to cancel the deal if you have to do so. Since Amazon always gives its sellers at least a week's time before running its, this is more than enough time to prevent cancellation situations.

Cancellations, in general, are not good. Even if you regularly cancel your Lightning Deals well in advance, Amazon might consider blacklisting you from submitting any Lightning Deals in the future. Therefore, evaluate all the scenarios beforehand and decide before you even create the deal.

If you do wish to cancel a deal, log in to your Lightning Deal Dashboard and browse through the All tab. Select the deal that you wish to cancel by clicking on View tab. Select Cancel Deal.

Get Product Reviews

More than 60 percent of online shoppers read online reviews before making their buying decisions. Reviews from real users of a product or service offer social proof of how good or bad it is; they provide a perception on the risk, if any. But the sad story for every seller is that only five to ten percent of customers leave a review for the product or service they buy. Experts and market researchers are still looking for the reason behind this fact.

The paradox is—no product reviews, no sales. No sales, no product reviews. And if a seller doesn't get reviews, he is trapped in a vicious cycle of Reviews <-> Sales and it becomes really important to break the cycle to be successful on Amazon. The good news is that there are some ways to get reviews in order to build credibility for your product.

- Offer something to your potential customers in exchange for product reviews. This is an effective, popular way of generating reviews for the product you are selling online. This concept is not new as there are several brands that give free gifts and samples to customers and influential marketers in exchange for their valuable reviews. In the same way that Amazon awards rankings to various listings based on its BSR system, it ranks reviewers based on the helpfulness of their reviews. Amazon gives away badges to top reviewers. The badges add value to their profile page, lending credibility and authenticity to their reviews.

- Look for review services that help you get reviews for your products. You can choose to go with this option if your product belongs to a very competitive category for which other sellers have many reviews in their listings. Be careful while using such services, though, as having too many reviews on your listing from those who received free samples from you is not seen as a good sign. Consumers complain against brands that try to boost their services by such means. There are several websites that can spot these fake reviews and ask customers to boycott them. Reviews are meant to add real value to the product that is being sold, not to misguide customers.
- Amazon's Vine Program helps its customers receive genuine reviews from some of the top reviewers in the industry. But the catch here is that the program is only for Vendors, and it's a paid program.
- Send follow-up emails to customers after they purchase your product. Sending post-purchase follow-up emails through Amazon's message system can also help in boosting your products' review rate. But if you send too many emails, it can be annoying. Therefore, write clear, concise emails and give customers a good reason to leave a review for your product. Make sure the email content is light, and humorous, if appropriate.

To launch and optimize your product listing:

- Prepare the plan to promote your product. Evaluate how many reviews you need as a baseline to get started with PPC advertising and other activities. 15-20 reviews are recommended for each product to start with as customers will see your listing as credible if you have at least that many reviews.

- Create an outreach plan. Start by preparing a list of top-ranked reviewers on Amazon and customers who have shown interest in your listing or have bought from you in the past. You can get their email addresses from their profile pages. Try to find at least 30-40 such customers; not everyone you contact will leave a review for your product. If you are busy with other aspects of your business, you can utilize review services to manage this part of your plan.

- If top-rated reviewers have never bought your products, send them samples. You can either utilize Amazon's FBA service or send them the product directly using your own shipping facility. Another option is a special coupon code that you can create for these reviewers on Amazon. Once you provide this code to the reviewer, the coupon system allows them to add your product to their cart for free. But if you choose to use this option, make sure your customer discloses the fact that they received the product from you for free. This is important in order not to violate the fair trade rules.

- Follow up with those to whom you sent a sample to make sure they write a review for you. The follow-up process can be tedious, but it is worth it if they write a review.

- Have a strategy to send post-purchase follow-up emails to your customers. Set up the sequence to enhance the number of reviews from your organic sales. You can either choose to send these emails manually or use Amazon's messaging service to do it for you.

Using Amazon Coupons

Another brilliant way to advertise your launch on Amazon is using its Coupon Codes to offer discounts to your customers. Your product has just arrived on the market, so you can give a discount to your loyal customers, family and friends so that they can spread the word and also leave a review for you. Amazon coupons are similar to those that you find in physical stores. You can utilize them to get a discount—dollars off, or a percentage off the selling price. Coupons, a simple and powerful tool to promote products, are available throughout the Amazon website including search results, detail pages, Gold Box Deal pages and landing pages. Since these are instantly applied, they help drive sales and are simple to use. There are a couple of things you can do with the coupon codes, but the two main uses are as discounts on your product and product launches. Based on your goals, you can decide how you want to use these codes.

There are two main types of coupons available on Amazon:

- Single-Use Coupons – These coupon codes can only be used once and are mainly used at the time of a product launch to avoid giving away discounted products to too many people.
- Regular Coupons – These coupons are available to everyone. Once created, anyone can use them

to get a discount. You really need to be careful with this type, or you might end up selling all your products at a discount.

How to Create Single-use Coupons:

1. Log in to your seller's account on Amazon.
2. Browse through the Promotions page by clicking on Advertising on the Home Page.
3. You can view various options to choose from but for creating single-use coupons, select Money Off.
4. Complete all the required fields.
   a. **Conditions**:

      Buyer Purchases: The buyer should fill this in to get the promotion. You can leave it unedited, but the "At Least this Quantity of Items" should be set at one.

      Purchase Items: Create a new product selection by choosing ASIN List from the options in the menu and clicking on Create Product Selection. Fill out the next one by leaving the first two slots blank. Under ASIN, input the ASIN of the product for which you want to offer the discount. Once you receive a success confirmation, return, refresh your browser and choose the product you just created by selecting it from the refreshed list.

      Buyer Gets: Choose how much of a discount you wish to offer on your product as part of this promotion. You can either give a flat amount off or offer a percentage discount. Using the Money Off option is your best bet to prevent the listing from being removed.

Applies to: State what the discount is good for. Choose "Purchase Items" from the drop-down list.

Buyer Benefit Applies to a Quantity of: Leave it as '1,' as you want the code to function just once, rather than multiple times.

Advanced Options: You can leave these options as-is.

b. **Scheduling:**

Start Date: Enter the date when the promotional code you are creating should activate. Click on the calendar icon that appears next to this field and select a start date. Note that it takes at least four hours for the coupon code to be activated no matter when you create it.

End Date: Enter the End Date when you want the coupon code to be no longer applicable.

Internal Description: Provide a name for your promotion code that relates to your listing so that it is easy for you to remember later.

Tracking ID: Leave it as-is.

c. **Additional Options:**
   This section is the most crucial one when it comes to selecting who is going to use your coupon code.

   Claim Code: To select the claim code, check the box. You will see a list of options in the drop-down list. Fill in the details.

   One redemption per customer: You should check this box as you are creating single-use codes.

   Claim Code: This is different from the other field we used. You will see the coupon code that people will use to get the discount on your product. However, as you are going to use the code just once, this code doesn't make any difference. Nevertheless, make a note of it.

   Claim Code Combinability: For this field, select the Exclusive option.

   Custom Messaging: You will see a drop-down list. Fill in all the required details and then scroll down to the bottom of the page and click Review.

d. **Confirm the Settings:**
   Review all the settings you have made to create the promotion. If all the details are correct, click on Confirm.

e. **Manage Promotions:**
   The promotion is created. Next, you need to create the codes. Go to the Manage Promotions section. To view the promotion you just created, click on Promotion Status and select All. You will see all the promotions. Select your promotion by clicking on the tracking ID.

f. **Manage Claim Codes:**
   Now you need to manage the codes. Click on the Manage Claim Codes tab and then click on Create and enter the Group Name and Quantity. You can download the code and save it wherever you want.

Job done! You have successfully created a single-use coupon code. Now all you need to do is to give this code to your customer and ask them to enter it at the time of checkout to get the discount on your product.

Using Amazon Vendor Express Account

Amazon Vendor Express allows sellers to share their products with millions of customers across the globe. Amazon buys products directly from sellers and is responsible for merchandising, shipping, returns and customer service. To have a Vendor Express account, you must have the intellectual property rights for the products you wish to sell on Amazon. If you don't own those rights, your product can still be considered for Amazon if it does not violate any third-party rights. The reasons someone would want to have a Vendor Express Account include:

- There are no annual charges to participate or join the program.
- To customers, the product appears as being sold by Amazon.
- Order handling and product storage are included.
- It includes free shipping of products from the seller's warehouse to Amazon or customers.
- It offers 24-hour returns and customer service.
- It provides automated pricing using advanced algorithms.
- Access to AMS (Amazon Marketing Services).

Products that are eligible for Vendor Express Account include:

- Appliances (parts and accessories)– Deep fryers, mixers, bread machine, food processors, coffee makers and espresso machines, etc.
- Arts and Crafts – Beading and jewelry-making items, painting supplies, craft kits, sewing accessories, knitting and crochet items, sewing boxes, etc.
- Beauty – Skincare, cosmetics, fragrance, suncare, etc.
- Bedding and Bath – Bath linens, bedding, curtains and blinds, inflatable beds, doormats, cushions, etc.

The most valuable thing you can gain from a Vendor Express Account is access to Amazon Market Services. The market services allow users to optimize content, access more robust reports and create ads. The

Sponsored Products offer a chance for vendors to pay Amazon only when your ad is clicked. However, there is one major difference of accessibility between Vendor Express and Vendor Central—Vendor Express doesn't provide access to A+ content, which is a premium feature that displays optimized vendors on the site. Because this account is more advanced than Seller Central in terms of PPC advertising, you must reap the full benefits by checking your campaign daily: Headline Search Ads, Sponsored Products and Product Display Ads.

You can also do a health check of your operational metrics by addressing chargebacks or issues related to inbound shipping, product packaging, etc. Some of your weekly tasks should include checking:

- Sales and Inventory – neatly displays your inventory levels.
- Cost of Goods Sold to Customers – displays a monthly picture of your sales.
- Purchase Orders – sets up a schedule to check your POs as this plays a crucial role in maintaining healthy account metrics.
- Product Pages – check your product pages every week and address all queries/concerns. This shows you respect and value your customers.

Some of your monthly tasks should include:

- Deep analyses of sales and inventory reports
- Marketing for your brand
- Product page audits

- Reports analyses – Once sales are settled for five to seven days, audit your sales and inventory reports to check the PO quantity, revenues and inventory trends. Develop a plan to ensure the trends are always moving up.
- Marketing – Vendor Express offers multiple marketing opportunities to evaluate your revenues, catalogue and determine promotional plans. You can create Lightning Deals, offer coupons and vendor-initiated price discounts to your potential customers.
- Product Page Audit – Plan and schedule your product page reviews to ensure they are optimized for A+ content, SEO, mobile devices and product reviews.

Amazon Brand Registry

As a seller on Amazon, you have your own brand that you are trying to sell. To protect your trademark and create trusted experiences for your customers, it is important that you utilize the Brand Registry provided by Amazon. The main goal is to make it simpler and easier for you to organize your brand. This helps you to:

- Protect your brand – Sellers always have a fear that their personal brands might get hijacked by nefarious merchants. As today's marketplace is really competitive, there are sellers who will go to any lengths to grow their businesses. The good news is that Amazon Brand Registry safeguards your brand by registering it so that you are the sole owner of the Buy Box for your brand. Even then, if at any time you feel someone is trying to hijack your brand and harm your reputation, you can get in touch with Amazon Customer Care to have the nefarious merchant removed from the platform.

- Have more control over your listings – If you're just a regular seller on Amazon, you have limited options and are restricted in how you define your listing. But if you opt for Amazon Brand Registry, you have some control in terms of product titles, product images, product details, product IDs issued by Amazon and so on.
- Have wider access to sell the product – There are several types of sellers who can opt for Amazon Brand Registry:
  1. those who create their own products
  2. those who create branded label products
  3. those who own private label brands and
  4. traditional manufacturers and distributors with permission to own the content of a brand on Amazon.

How to register and list products: Amazon can take up to two weeks to complete the whole Brand Registry approval process, provided you have submitted all the information that Amazon requires about your brand. Two things that help you get approval are the Brand Name and Key Attribute Value. You need to provide a picture of each product that displays its packing and branding, the product itself and a link to where you have been selling your product so far. Consider key attributes you will be using such as the model number of the product, catalogue number, manufacturer part number or style number. Make your decision based on attributes that remain the same and which are easily identifiable to your customers and distributors. Once you have been approved for the Brand Registry, you can start listing.

Brand Name: Be very careful when mentioning your brand name. Spell it correctly and write it exactly how you want it to be because that's how it will be referred to by Amazon.

Key Attribute Value: Choose a key attribute value from the list mentioned, and whatever you choose, use it for all your products. But each product should have a unique value.

IMPORTANT: You need to have a trademark registered if you want to be brand registered. It takes about six months to file an application and have it approved. Once it is approved, you can enroll with Brand Registry by browsing through the Brand Registry page of Amazon and selecting Enroll a New Brand. Then, complete a three-step application process:

1. Fill in details for Brand eligibility. Enter the trademark registration or the serial number and state "Registered With" by selecting an appropriate entry from the drop-down menu.
2. Upload your packaging, product and logo images by following the image requirements mentioned on the page. As part of this step, you are also required to focus on your online presence. Mention your Brand website and Brand social media page.
3. Fill in the characteristics section of the Brand Registry application.

Optimizing your Listings

Online shoppers, especially those who generally shop on Amazon, decide within a few seconds if they want to go back to the search results or engage with the detail page further. Here, you have an opportunity to win visitors' hearts so that they check all the details about your product and ultimately buy your product.

Titles do matter – Most sellers do not pay much attention to the titles they create on their description page. The fact is, titles plays an important role in getting sales. Make sure the title you use clearly describes what you are trying to sell and meets a customer's needs. Also mention your brand name so that customers recognize you. The title shouldn't be too long and needs to clarify the main use or primary benefit of the product.

Bullet points are your best pitch factor – Bullet points are really important as they help the customers skim over the section and see key details about the product. Mention all the key points as bullets so that the customer doesn't have to look for information elsewhere. Some of the key points that you must talk about include customer service or any available warranty for a product. Also make sure the bullets are really short and to-the-point.

Pictures play a key role in the game: Shoppers usually make their buying decision on the basis of the product's image. It is therefore important that your main display image shows the product clearly, with or without panning/zooming. If you have additional images, these should display different angles of the product. It is also good to have one picture that just shows the back of the product indicating instructions, ingredients, etc.

Product Description is no less important: I hope you remember that your customers, for the most part, are skimming through the listing, and if you have a lengthy description, they will just skip it. Instead, use a brand voice and highlight key selling points while providing facts to support your statements. This will help customers understand why they should choose your product over a competitor's.

Facebook Ads to Uplift Your Sales

Being the fastest and largest growing online medium, Facebook is the standard for gauging various social traffic generating sources today. With more than 1.39 billion users, it's a hive with plenty of opportunities and activities for all sorts of businesses and sellers. One of Facebook's most amazing features is Facebook Ads. Getting clicks is good, but what really drives sales is conversions and Facebook Ads help optimize listings for conversions. Trust me; if you are not targeting this feature of Facebook, you are missing out something big.

Try Facebook advertising to reach out to new customers and keep the existing ones engaged. This is what most e-commerce firms, leading brands and Amazon sellers do to generate traffic to their listings or sites. According to studies, businesses are able to attract up to 70 percent of their traffic through the social channel. With well-designed, well-optimized programs, businesses have managed to make up to seven times the returns on their ads. Social marketing is here to stay, so utilize the power of Facebook advertising to see some good numbers for your business!

Amazon sellers love utilizing the Facebook advertising platform to market their products because of Facebook's targeting capabilities. Its user base, which is quite interesting and attractive, is capable of identifying and targeting segments that make it extremely effective. Facebook has the built-in capability to collect massive data from all its audiences, which helps marketers target specific audiences.

Marketing on Facebook is user-friendly, straightforward, flexible and powerful. With only basic knowledge, one can easily create and run campaigns, achieving a good return on investments. Therefore, this social platform is seen as a goldmine for e-commerce sellers, particularly those who are looking to generate more and more traffic to their sites. The medium not only offers them good profits and returns but also gives their organic ranking an effective means to increase conversion rates and sales velocity. Facebook gives its customers an edge over other competitors in the market. Various sellers who use Facebook for their marketing purposes have experienced great results from their businesses on Amazon.

Newcomers to Amazon and/or Facebook are concerned about the cost factor, the difficulty level and the time required to learn how to use the platform. But the reality is that Facebook Ads are really simple and easy to set up. So, let's have a look at the basics of how you can drive more sales with Facebook Ads. Once you have the basic know-how, you can explore further on your own and see how these campaigns can be created to achieve your marketing goals.

Create Your Business Page on Facebook

Creating a business page on Facebook is quite simple and straightforward. The entire process is four basic steps:

1. Log into your account and create a new page by navigating to the right-hand corner of your dashboard and selecting Create a Page from the drop-down menu.
2. Choose a category based on the type of your business. You can see various categories of businesses, so select one Brand or Product that most suits you as an Amazon FBA seller.
3. Select an industry-specific category that closely matches your industry-specific business. Fill in all the basic details in the fields under this category. Accept all the terms and conditions on the Facebook pages and then Get Started.
4. Now launch the page and optimize it. Add a compelling description that helps your customers know your brand. Add a link to your listing or store. Upload good quality pictures. Click on the option that says Reach More People so that you have improved visibility to potential customers. Once done, you can bookmark this page so that you can regularly visit and check for updates.

Set up your Ads Account

You are just one step away from creating ads on Facebook. All you need is to provide your personal and professional details to Facebook, then enter all the required information so that your campaigns can be funded.

- Browse through the Adverts Manager by selecting either Adverts Manager or Create Advert from your account.
- Add all the information on the settings page by selecting Settings. Choose the option that says you will utilize Facebook Ads for your business. Carefully fill in all other required details; once submitted, these details cannot be edited later. Entering your correct address is important as you will be contacted at this address for all billing related tasks/updates.
- Fill in the billing information by clicking on Billing from the left-hand menu. Now navigate to Payment Method and click on Add New Payment Method. Based on how you will be making payments, enter your PayPal or credit card details for funding purposes.

  If you add a credit card as your payment method, make sure you have a sufficient credit limit. If you don't, your campaigns will go nowhere until you increase the credit limit or pay the outstanding amount. You should keep a backup payment ready so that your funding can always be taken care of.

Key Ad Types and Variables

Facebook offers a variety of ad types, but for now, we will be focusing only on the ones that are valid for Amazon.

Page Boost Ads: These ads enhance the visibility of your link post-photo update.

Page Posts Video Ads: These ads show a muted video ad until it is tapped.

Carousel Ads or Multi-product: These ads showcase different variations of audiences or a catalogue of products. This format shows up to ten images or videos, links, headlines or call-to-action.

The current trend in the marketplace for the most economical form of getting clicks is through video ads that are targeted to phone users. But this is not always the case as it is difficult to provide precise information on how these ads can be shown since each product functions uniquely. So, you must always try it out.

Ad Creation on Facebook

You can start creating ads on Facebook in three ways:

1. **Your Facebook page**: Clicking boosts the posts to a wider audience. This is generally not recommended.
2. **Ads Manager** offers additional functions and is user-friendly.
3. **Power Editor** offers the most advanced features and interface.

Using Power Editor is the best way create ads on Facebook, and it is not too difficult or time-consuming to learn the advanced features it offers. The best thing about this method is that Power Editor is really handy when you want to do split testing, create bulk ads or create more than one campaign with different budgets and targeted audiences. Keep an eye on the various mechanisms as Facebook is always updating and coming up with changes.

Facebook segregates the ad creation process into three components: Campaigns (the objective of overall ad creation process), Ad Sets (sets within the main ads) and Ads (creative, individual adverts).

- A **Campaign** can have multiple Ad Sets but a unique campaign objective. Consider a campaign like a container that helps you organize your advertising better. The only attribute associated with it is the objective you want to attain. Therefore, if you want to increase the number of likes on your page or drive more sales to your site, you need to create two separate campaigns (one per objective).
- An **Ad Set** can have multiple ads contained within it but has a unique schedule, audience targeting, placement and budget. They are considered as the best units to perform A/B testing.
- An **Ad** is the smallest unit of a Facebook campaign. Ads can contain ad images, URLs, etc. The sub-groups and groups can be utilized to create various campaign features but when the objective of a campaign changes, it impacts all

the ads contained within that campaign. if you change the budget for your Ad Set, it will be reflected in the ads created within that specific group.

Objectives – Clearly establishing your marketing objectives helps the platform understand what your goal is in creating the ad. Accordingly, Facebook can then automatically help you improvise the ads by showing the ads to a target audience. Currently, Facebook offers several objectives for ad creation and it is regularly adding more:

- **Clicks to the website:** Visitors click on your ad and reach your listing/site.
- **Website conversion:** Visitors reach your goal page, such as an order completion page on your website.
- **Page post engagement:** Visitors get connected with your posts by commenting, liking and sharing them.
- **Page likes:** increasing the number of page likes.
- **Offer claims:** offering and promoting a product deal or discount.
- **Video views:** getting more views on your videos.
- **Dynamic product ads:** retargeting users to your page and promoting the product.

You can choose to go with any one of these ad objectives based on your goals, but you will have to pay for the kind of traffic your ad receives. Facebook will help you by showing your ads to those who are capable of meeting the defined objective.

If you want a Facebook ad to lead to purchases and email sign-ups, you can go with website conversion as your objective. But on the other hand, if your focus is on building your fan base on Facebook, you might want to look at the Page Likes option. Your main objective as a seller is to drive sales to your site, but unfortunately no single ad type, objective type or tactic can guarantee this. Like every visitor, every brand is unique, and you might have to try out different approaches to see which one works the best for you. It is always good to explore, and also to keep a constant check on the competitors. However, when choosing the apt objective for your business, experts believe that ads with low-friction conversion generally do great. Therefore, offering a discount coupon and asking for an email sign-up in return is an effective way to market your business on this platform.

Audience – Your ad can be directed to the selected audience by using an array of targeting options. Hence, it is worth exploring options and trying them out before shortlisting one. Some of these options include location, gender, age, relationship, work, education, interests, life events, hobbies, behaviors, language and connections, etc.

Choose some of the targeting options and then try them out in opposition to each other. For example, target five interests for one audience and build five different audiences with their ad sets to understand which one is the best. You can also choose to create custom audiences by targeting audiences of users through their existing contact lists, email lists, etc. This is an effective tool, particularly for advanced marketers who are looking to exclude or target specific audiences.

Types of Audiences

Facebook offers primarily three types of audience types:

Saved Audience: Set up a saved audience in the campaign setup phase or in the Audience Manager. If you look at the window, you are required to include targeting. Facebook allows to you target an audience based on location (country, state, city, postal code etc.); demographics (age, gender, language etc.); interests (apps they use, hobbies, pages they like or share, likes and interests etc.) and behavior (purchase history, specific events like anniversaries, etc.)

Custom Audience: This is probably the most highly-valued target audience as it retargets past visitors and those who have engaged with you before. You can create custom audiences using customer files, website traffic, app activity or engagement. If you choose to create an audience based on existing files, whether you use their phone numbers, email addresses or app IDs, you can click on Create a Facebook Custom Audience and then select the Custom File. Import the file that has your customer data and then upload it.

Next, if you want to create your ad based on website traffic, which allows you to create remarketing campaigns for those who have engaged with you, just log in to Audience Manager and select Website Traffic.

You can choose targets from the drop-down list. If you want to reach an audience based on App Activity, target people who are involved in specific actions in your app. Lastly, if you want to create a set based on engagement, you can target those who visited your Facebook page, those who were engaged with your page posts on Facebook, sent you a message on your page, clicked on any of the call-to-action buttons or saved any of your pages or posts.

Lookalike Audiences: You can even create a Lookalike Audience set from customers that resemble the existing list. To create this kind of a set, you first need to build a custom audience set to tell Facebook that these are the types of users you are trying to target. Based on this, your lookalike audience set will be created. From the Creation menu, select a target country and the percentage of users from the targeted country. This percentage signifies the audiences similar to the selected custom audience.

Another advantage that Facebook offers FBA sellers is that they have access to the database of customer contact numbers. These details can be plugged into Facebook to create a custom audience list for promoting new products as well as retargeting the current list of customers.

Now let us look at the next attribute.

Ad Placement: Just creating the ads is not enough; placing them in a way that most users see them is even more important. Facebook gives its users the liberty to display the ads in different formats and positions, which include placing ads on the sidebar, mobile ads, desktop ads in the newsfeed and so on. The majority of Facebook users use a mobile app, and this group is expanding. In several instances, mobile ads have outperformed their desktop counterparts, especially with click-through-rates. Hence, it is important that you make sure your website or landing page is mobile-friendly in order to reap some of the best results.

In terms of desktop ads, Facebook gives you two placements options—ads on the sidebar and in the newsfeed. Although you do not need a Facebook page if you go with the sidebar option, it is comparatively less effective at driving traffic as compared to the newsfeed option.

If you are confused about how much to spend on your Facebook Ads, setting up a daily budget for your ads will help you control your budget. Another option is to set ads up in a way that they run continuously with specified start and/or end dates. In nascent stages, when you are not sure about your budget, it is good to test the results of your ads by setting the budget in the range of $5 to $10. Gather and analyze the results from your ads and then move ahead accordingly.

Optimize and Gain control over Bidding: Facebook allows you to set a budget and then automatic bidding to do the rest. You can base your bidding on Cost-Per-Click or Cost-Per-1000 impressions. Apply new ideas by varying your daily budget, controlling bids, total budget and other attributes and analyzing the risks based on these factors. This way you can test the engagement of your audience by setting up low budgets before you decide to scale up. A great benefit that Facebook offers its users is it automatically bids for space and optimizes your ad to suit the objective you have selected. You can choose to leave these settings as-is at least until you are well-acquainted with the entire process.

Manual vs. Automatic Bidding: If you are new to the Facebook Advertising world, start with Automatic bidding as this doesn't require you to have any prior knowledge about average cost per result or average bid.

If you are well aware of the results and the value to your business, use Manual bidding. For instance, if you are trying to optimize your Ad Set for clicks on your link, you can set any price you want for the link clicks. If you are trying to set the value, Facebook will show you the suggested range, so change it as per your needs.

Reporting and Analysis: This is another great feature that Facebook provides its users. Once you complete setting up your ad and submit it, Facebook will approve and launch it. You can then monitor the performance through the Ads Manager reports in real time. Allow your campaign to run at least a few days before drawing any conclusions. Once the campaign runs for a few days, Facebook's data collection will provide vital insights into the performance as well as the target audience; these results are provided in a tabular format based on your objective. Some of the most important metrics include:

- Reach – number of users who have seen the ad
- Conversions – number of users who reach the desired action

- Cost – needed per desired action
- Click-through-rate – number of users who clicked on the ad and
- Frequency – average number of times a single user saw your ad.

Comparing these numbers to identify the best performers will help you think of more profitable ideas and ads for the future.

Apart from the campaign metrics you will see in the Ads Manager report, you can take it one step further by using the Breakdown menu available. This way you can break down the reports by:

- Delivery_– age, location, gender, platform, device, etc.
- Action_– destination, video view type, video sound, etc.
- Time – week, days, month, etc.

Using a campaign breakdown, you can understand which ad placements perform the best, what are the best performing targets and what times of the day deliver the best conversion rates.

AMZPromoter: This feature integrates your ads to help you easily build a great converting landing page. You have two options in terms of where your customers are diverted when they click on your ad on Facebook—either send them to your listing directly or send them to an intermediary landing page first and then to the product page. I strongly recommend going with the second option. This is why:

- Your conversion rate will be much higher as your leads are qualified before they are diverted to your listing.
- You can easily capture email addresses, which is a great asset in building a customer list.
- You can offer a coupon code to your potential customers as this reduces the likelihood of them purchasing another similar product.
- You can add the conversion code to the intermediary page as this helps you in building your pixel on Facebook (discussed in the following section) and assists you in retargeting audiences on Google and Facebook.

To help you achieve this, AMZPromoter simplifies the whole process. With this tool, you can build a landing page that offers a high conversion rate with just a few clicks, as most of the fields are pre-filled using Amazon API. To build it, you just need to include your ASIN, add your coupons and select your landing page. Once the landing page is created, you will be provided with a unique URL that can be used to divert all traffic, or you will be given a code snippet that allows you to embed the landing page on your domain.

Once you have an intermediary landing page, remember to direct your customers to it as you are setting up your ad on Facebook. This landing page will have an opt-in button, which, when clicked, asks customers to enter their email addresses. Once the email address is entered, the customer will be redirected to another page where they can claim their discount coupon. On this coupon page there will be instructions on how to use the coupon and a link that takes the customer to your Amazon product page. Job accomplished!

Start creating your Facebook Ads, interface these ads with the Promoter and drive more traffic to your product page.

Ad Objectives and Facebook Pixel

Facebook Ads have become the go-to marketing platform for businesses and e-commerce sites. Facebook constantly keeps updating to improve its customer base. This allows retargeting based on increased targeting capabilities and various factors so that users can target a specific audience that is likely to buy the product. In this manner, advertisers have managed to decrease their acquisition costs by around 75 percent. How? Here's an example. You are selling a vegetable spiral slicer. For this product, your target audience will not just include those who love to cook, but particularly those who love to cook western dishes. You can narrow your search and get so granular that you can target the exact audience.

With billions of active users, Facebook Ads can help Amazon sellers to drive quality traffic to their listing. However, in order to see the real sales, it all comes down to understanding who the real audiences are and how you can reach them through these ads and advertising objectives. In our last section, we discussed advertising objectives—the actions you want people to take when they come across your ads. The following three objectives should be in line with your goals of exactly what you expect from your ads:

Awareness: Create the awareness of what interest your product should generate such as brand awareness or local area awareness.

Consideration: Lead your audience to consider your product and look for more details about it. This can include video views, views, traffic, lead generation, app installations and engagement.

Conversions: This objective is optimized for those who are likely to make a purchase. Using the power of Pixel (discussed later in this chapter), you can display your ad in front of audiences who are likely to buy your product.

As an Amazon seller, you must mainly focus on these objectives:

- **Pay Per Engagement**: Pay Per Engagement, or PPE ads, offer the least expensive method to boost customer engagement and reach on Facebook. These ads are optimized to be displayed in front of those who are likely to engage with your posts. The engagement can be in the form of post clicks, post likes, page likes, link clicks, shares and/or comments. It is an effective means to gain insight and analyze whether you are targeting the right audience or if there is a need to scale up your ad. PPE ads can be in the form of a video, photo or presentation created within the Ads Manager platform. You can create the ad using a post on your FB page, boosting it within the Ads Manager tool. It is important that you consider virality when creating these ads, as they are most effective when the content is shareable. PPE ads are a valuable asset to measure how responsive and effective your ads are.

- **Clicks to Website**: Clicks to Website or CTW are the ads optimized to show to those who are likely to click your ad. Based on the relevance and targeting of your ad, you will have to pay a variable amount each time someone clicks on the link in your ad. The aim is to build pixel data for Amazon sellers. Apart from this, you will get sales if customers find your product interesting. However, though these ads will be shown to those who are likely to click the ad, they might not purchase your product. So, at this time, your aim should be to get the attention of customers. If you integrate CTW with AMZPromoter, you can get valuable data about your potential customers in the form of their email addresses.

- **Website Conversions**: This is where you can actually make money from your ads. Once you have done your job of figuring out the ad and targeting (with the help of PPE ads), and you have also created some pixel data (with the help of CTW ads), you are all set to dive into the pool of website conversions. These are the ads optimized for pixel data. If you own a website, you will have a main pixel on the site and another conversion pixel on your payment page, product page, purchase page and so on. Don't worry. You do not have to create these pixels yourself; Facebook has done all the groundwork and provides you with the standard pixel code. All you need to do is copy the event code into the main code and then paste it on the required pages. In case you have integrated AMZPromoter, paste the primary pixel to the landing page and cart conversion pixel to the coupon page.

Facebook Pixel: Facebook Pixel is a code that, when installed on a specific page, sends the message to Facebook when someone clicks, visits or takes action. It is a website plug-in that measures how effective your advertisement is by understanding the actions people take on that webpage. If you are serious about selling on Amazon, you should utilize this Facebook feature as it helps you measure and optimize your ads to build a customer base. It also allows you to:

- track your conversions
- optimize your ads for better conversion rate
- build a customer base

Setting up the pixel lets you:

- target people based on content engagement
- target people who visited your landing page or site
- target people who visited your listing but didn't buy your product
- optimize ads and display them to those who are likely to buy your product

- track those conversions. Using pixels helps you measure the conversions so you can evaluate your return on the investment you made in the ads. You can see if the amount you are spending is worthwhile and if not, can optimize it.

How to use a pixel: You can use this feature of Facebook in two scenarios— if you have set up a custom conversion or if you are running any of the following predefined Facebook events:

Events

- View Content – when a visitor lands on a page of your website.
- Search – when someone uses the search feature to look for something on your website.
- Add to Cart – when a visitor adds something to his cart on your website.
- Add to Wishlist – when a visitor adds something to his wish list on your website.
- Initiate Checkout – when someone initiates the checkout process to purchase something from your website.
- Make Purchase – when someone completes the purchase process on your website.
- Add Payment info – when someone enters payment information to buy something from your website.

- Lead – when someone identifies himself as a lead on your website.
- Complete registration – when someone completes the registration process on your website.

Custom Conversions

If instead of the nine events mentioned above, you want to use custom conversions to collect more details than what these events can provide, this is how you can do it. Custom conversions use a rule based on certain URL keywords or URLs, and instead of tracking all records using the standard event View Content, you can use pixel tracking to view records of a specific category. But before you use Facebook Pixel, you will have to make the platform understand the details of your conversion event that you are going to track:

- browse through Facebook Ads Manager and click on Custom Conversions.
- click on Create Custom Conversions to define your custom event using the specific URL rules. You can even create these custom conversion events by adding more details to the standard FB events. These additional bits are called parameters, and they help you to customize your events based on a specific search string, a product name or category, the number of items someone adds to his or her cart and so on.

Track your Facebook Ads with Google Analytics

Google Analytics is considered one of the best market analytics tools available, regardless of the nature and size of your business, industry or technical expertise. It is a tool that can truly help you track the success of your Facebook Ads and campaigns.

If you can successfully track conversions, it's a big achievement, and analyzing what touchpoints to assign the most weight to is crucial. If you are able to view the entire path to those conversions along with the converted ad, it will help improve your return on investment and overall success. This will give you good insight into what your customers are looking for. You will be able to see what it is that specific set of audiences are finding useful on your website. If you choose to run a campaign and track users throughout the journey, it will help you identify the niches within your domain that you can target more accurately with new campaigns and more highly-targeted messages.

Being able to understand what your audience's expectations are before and after the ad conversion can help you make sure the conversion path is optimized for relevant items; you can always view the biggest hits on your content. Last, but not least, you can gain insight into your audience base. While you can use Audience Insights to learn about your audience, Google Analytics can present you with some astonishing results when you see who is actually converting outside your fan circle—this might be very different from what you had expected. Business owners and marketers have been observing for quite some time now that in the process of calculating conversions from your Facebook Ads, the measurements provided by analytics websites and Ads Manager are quite different from the numbers given by Google Analytics. It's important to try to understand why the results are different and which is the more reliable source.

The main reason the two platforms show different results is because they track the data differently. Facebook's default conversion process through conversions and click-through conversions is not the same as Google's. There are two different types of conversions:

- View-Through Conversions – when a visitor sees the ad but doesn't click, although he still visits the website and converts
- Click-Through Conversions – when a visitor clicks on the ad and converts

Facebook's analysis for Click-Through Conversions is performed on an ad within 28 days, and for the View-Through Conversions, in just one day. It also gives credit to the first page the visitor lands on during the process of conversion, although the visitor can view various pages before buying your product.

On the other hand, Google Analytics gives credit to the last touchpoint in the process of conversion. Hence, the numbers will be different than what Facebook provides. Google also gives its users a system that lets them select the way they wish to distribute the credit for the conversion. This way a seller can weigh different touchpoints the visitor came across before buying the product and assign different weights.

How to Track Facebook Ads Using Google

When you run ads on Facebook that point to your site or page, the traffic is tracked by Google Analytics. This also takes into account the users who click through non-paid posts on your Facebook page. Therefore, there is a need to explicitly filter out this traffic through non-paid postings from your Facebook Ads as you wish to know how your ads are performing. This can be done as follows:

- Create a link which is trackable – This can be done quickly and easily if you are using AdEspresso. You will have to enter the source, medium, name of the campaign and content. You can then enter which content you want to feed to Analytics from the drop-down option under Placeholder. You can add parameters like Ad Id, Ad Set Name, Campaign Id, Age, etc. Once this is done, these parameters will be added to the ads as a traceable link and you can see the data in your Google Analytics account.

  Browse through Acquisition and then click on Campaign. This way, the placeholders can be quickly and easily included in the campaign as compared to manually creating links using a URL builder tool. You can also build split tests within the campaign on parameters like location and age to see which location is providing the best conversion, or which age group is staying longest on your page.

If you choose to use Google's URL Builder to create the trackable link, you first need to enter some information such as your website's URL, source, medium, etc. Once this is done, Google will provide you with a long URL that should be copied and pasted into the Ads Manager.

- Check the results in Google Analytics. You have entered all the required parameters, so now you must wait for the data to be updated in Google Analytics. This can be viewed using Source or Campaign Name and will let you see the how well your ad is doing on the website.

Now, let's look at some additional tracking features for your ad. Apart from performance, Google Analytics lets you track your goals, sales, things occurring on your website, etc. You can use this data to analyze your return on investment from these ads.

Track

This is one of the tools that allow you to track your goals. Enter a goal. For example, you can enter the contact page of your website as the end goal. Add a Funnel that tracks the trajectory a visitor takes before buying your product. Once you set it up, you can verify it and know your conversion rate.

Attribution

You can tailor your attribute models in Google Analytics by either setting up goals or tracking the business. To create a custom model, you first need to select the type of model, and your options are as follows:

- Linear – gives equal distribution to all touchpoints.
- First interaction – offers the most credit to the first engagement point for the conversion, but the attribution for other sites remains equal.
- Last interaction – gives credit to the last engagement point for the conversion, but the attribution for the other sites remains equal.
- Time decay – gives the most credit to the last engagement point for the conversion and offers time decay attribution to each of the touchpoints.
- Position based – gives the maximum credit to the first and last engagement point for the conversion.

You can then compare the data for the different models to get a complete picture of various touchpoints that generate sales for your ads on Facebook; you can also view the path visitors are taking in the conversion process.

Must-Have Marketing Tools on Facebook

There are seven marketing tools that you can implement on Facebook:

Facebook Offers: When you make a product or service more exclusive, chances are you are increasing interest in them and, therefore, sales. This is because people, especially those with a lot of spending money, are not happy about being excluded from a group, even if they were not interested in it in the first place! They like to be a part of something that they think only a few others should be included in. Similar to Google Offers Extensions, Facebook Offer is a tool that you can use to announce and implement short-term, exclusive sales for a select few customers or members of your target audience. If this goes well, then you can think about implementing the offered scheme on a large-scale basis for more revenue.

The Classic Ads: Facebook primarily earns its revenue from the popularity it has that companies or people want to cash in on by posting their ads on Facebook. People all around the world who use Facebook will see a number of traditional ads on one side of their Facebook page, depending on the device they use. The ads will appear in a different area on smartphones as compared to its position on laptops or tablets.

Promoted Posts: Facebook has an option to make your posts more popular than they already are. All you need to do is choose the option Promote Post when you post something on your business account, choose the people you want the post to be highlighted for, specify what amount you can pay for this service and Facebook will do the rest. This will help you know how many people your post will reach (just the people who like your page and their friends in their Facebook Friends list), how long this promotion will last and what your payment options are.

Sponsored content: Many people use Facebook primarily for informative or social purposes. They don't have products or services in mind when they are browsing through their Facebook pages. If a person likes or shares your business page or a post, it will be highlighted to their friends in the form of a Sponsored Ad or Sponsored Post. In this way, people get to know what products or services their friends like and, should your content be good enough, they too can become a part of your customer group.

Facebook Exchange: We often see that people who start buying something online, or even at a store, change their minds in the middle of a decision and do not complete the transaction. There may be a number of reasons for this, and it's not always the fault of the business, the product or the service in question. A customer may be very preoccupied with personal issues, for example, so the transaction does not get completed. With the help of Facebook Exchange, you can gently prompt customers about an item that they once expressed interest in but did not complete the transaction for. Facebook and business entities have a legal understanding that allows businesses to inform Facebook about the times or places when a transaction on their website was canceled (based on analytical tools and data) so that Facebook can market that particular product or service the next time that person is on their site.

Facebook Insights: Facebook allows people who create and manage a page on their site to see how well a post was received, how many times it was shared, what the amount of negative impact it created was and how many clicks and backlinks it was able to generate. Each of these items plays a very important role in measuring how much interest and marketability your business has, so you can use this data to improve your marketing strategies.

Third-party apps: There are a number of third-party apps that you can purchase or install for free such as Agora Pulse, EdgeRank Checker by Social Bakers, ShortStack from Facebook, Facebook Page Barometer, AgoraPulse Contest, Conversation Store, Likealyzer, FanPage Karma from Facebook and Wolfram Alpha Personal Analytics. These apps are used to analyze the way your page has performed over a specific period of time, the demographics and frequency of the number of likes your posts have received, etc. Adding these apps to your Facebook page will help you analyze the performance of your page so that you can improve on the weaker areas and decide if there are other marketing tools or services that you need to invest in. There are also apps that help you keep track of your competitors' posts and the interest that they have generated so you can compare your performance with a similar company.

Get to the Real Work: Creating a Facebook Page

Setting up a business page for your brand is fairly easy once you are ready with the necessary information. The following instructions walk you through the steps to create a business page on Facebook. Note that you will have to be logged into Facebook with your company/brand profile before following these steps:

1. Once you've logged in and are on the homepage of your Facebook screen, scroll down to the bottom of the screen and click on the advertising link. The link will lead you to useful information on business pages and their effectiveness. It also provides tips that help you make the most of your Facebook page.
2. Click the button positioned on the middle left corner of the screen that reads Create a Page. Once you've done so, a Facebook wizard will take you through the following steps.
3. Select a category that best defines your line of business. We have already discussed the three categories available on the website. Recognize the category that your business fits into and select one of the mentioned options:
   - Local business – Internet cafés, pizza joints, travel and advertising firms, etc.
   - Brand, Product or Organizations – software companies, airlines, nonprofit organizations, etc.
   - Artist, Bands or Public figures – actors, musicians and politicians.

It's important that you take time to correctly identify your line of work. Every category mentioned above has a unique marketing template and uses specific tools for specific purposes. Choosing the wrong category can jeopardize your marketing strategies because you will be using the wrong tools in the first place. For example, a brand category will utilize different dynamics when compared to the local and public figure categories.

4. Next, fill in your business name in the field that reads Name of Another Business Field. This will be the name of your Facebook page. Click Get Started.

   Note that the name remains permanent and will be the face of your brand and company. Therefore, select a name that resonates with your line of business as this will be seen by all Facebook users. This name will also be a part of your Facebook page address. So think creatively and come up with a name that you want to be known by. By default, when you create a page, you become its administrator and hold the right to make changes to it. You also automatically become its first fan. However, any interaction you make when logged in as administrator will represent the brand of the business and not you as an individual. Similarly, any interactions you make as a fan will be displayed as comments by a fan and will be external to your company's page. In addition to this, people visiting your page and liking it will automatically become fans of your page. When you acquire more than 1000 fans of your page, Facebook rewards you with a prime URL on Facebook.

5. Fill in the credentials and check the box to certify that you are authorized to create the page. Type in your full name as the electronic signature.

6. Add a description describing the company. You may also choose to add a profile picture for identification purposes.

7. Lastly, once you've checked that the credentials entered are accurate and precise, click the button that reads Create the Page. You will be prompted with a congratulatory message stating you have successfully created the page. Note: Your page remains inactive and open for editing until you chose to publish it.

8. Once you are satisfied with the general layout and information listed on the page, click Publish to make it visible to the public.

Tailoring Your Facebook Page

Facebook encourages you to be creative and allows you to customize your page uniquely. Other than a few guarded restrictions, the website doesn't restrict your creativity in any way. For example, let's say you wish to change the order of the events listed on your page. Thanks to a sleek technology called "AJAX" (Asynchronous JavaScript and XML), you simply have to click the event or item bar and drag it to your desired new location. Everything other than the photo listed on the top left corner of the screen will be moved to the new location. How simple is that?

Uploading a Picture

The first thing to do to customize your page is to give it a face people can look at. Uploading a picture that represents your company logo or product will help Facebook users and fans visiting your page to identify with it. Remember that more often than not, visual and graphical representation stay longer in people's memory than text and information. Facebook allows you to upload images and photos in JPG, GIF and PNG format only. The pictures can be sized at 396 pixels in width and a height that is three times higher than the width. In addition to this, the maximum file size for an image is capped at 4 MB.

To upload a photo or image on your Facebook business page:

1. Log into your page and click on the prominent question mark seen at the top of the screen.
2. Click on the change picture link. The link will take you to a screen where you can view and edit your profile picture.
3. Click on the Upload Photo button.
4. Browse the picture you want to upload and open it from the location where it is stored.
5. Double click on the photo or click open to initialize the process of uploading photo.
6. Fill in information to describe the photo. This will be displayed on the wall of your profile and can be viewed by everyone. So be creative and come up with an attractive and captivating description. You can also choose to skip this step and proceed further.
7. Once you have verified all information and are satisfied with the image and description, select Publish to make your image and description visible to all.

Understanding TAB functions

Info tab: Information listed in this tab varies with the category and business type you choose. However, in general, the tab consists of two sections: basic info and detailed info. The basic info displays information, such as your contact details and business hours. The detailed info displays information on the website address, company overview, vision, mission, and any future forecasts as well the line of products or service you offer.

Your Facebook page increases your chances of being sourced among the top results in your field. Therefore, to increase your search engine optimization, enter keywords that you know will be typed in to pull up relevant information.

Wall tab: The wall is where the entire buzz is happening. You can share thoughts, ideas and messages that you want to share with fans and visitors to your page. Whether it is an idea you wish to incorporate, a mere thought reflecting your views on a specific topic or interactions with fans and visitors to your page, the wall is the ideal platform for it all. It allows you to broadcast your message and be heard in an instant.

The wall displays your messages and broadcasts them as stories for people visiting your page. So keep it active and buzzing. You can post links to blogs you've written on a product or service or post questions and ask for suggestions. Make sure you keep the audience engaged for this is what keeps interests levels high and has them coming back for more. Here's a list of ideas and content you can use to update your wall:

✓ Social content: Share a message of up to 365 characters in length on either a social content or an event in your line of business.
✓ Links: Share links to blogs, newsfeeds from your website or interesting reads on relevant topics.
✓ Photos: Create a storyboard of sorts and share photos. You can upload photos of events, product launches and team outings. While single photos can be uploaded, you can also group multiple photos to create an album.
✓ Videos: Create and upload a video for a review or launch. This will portray your skills and knowledge of the subject and will further contribute to your credibility.

Photos tab: The photos tab is specifically meant for uploading photos to your page. Create albums and storyboards that share memories of a milestone event.

Keep it fresh and interesting. Regularly refresh your profile pictures with relevant images of products and updates. You can also re-order and rotate images to make them look fresh and prominent. To gain visibility and reach, you can tag people who are featured in a photo. This will help you create a viral chain of people linked to that image. When tagged, people on their pages see the image and will indirectly get a glimpse of your company's profile. To upload a photo in the photo tab:

1. Click the photo tab.

2. Click the button that reads Add Photo Album. You can name the album, identify the location and include short descriptions to illustrate the album.
3. Click the button that reads Create an Album.
4. Browse and open the photo or album you want to upload.
5. Click Upload.

Discussion tab: This tab lets you discuss, debate and share ideas, questions and suggestions with your fans. Think of this as an online survey to gauge and identify your customers' feedback and suggestions on your products or services. To access the Discussions tab:

1. Click the Discussion Tab on your Facebook screen.
2. Click on the button that reads Start a New Topic.
3. Write the content you wish to discuss, and initiate a conversation.

Considering that discussions can run into pages and be spread over various topics, Facebook allows you to view discussions based on topics. To view the discussions on a specific topic:

1. Go to View Topic.
2. Select the topic name and start viewing.

Facebook displays the conversations relevant to the specified topic. In addition to this, you can contribute your views by sharing, liking and replying to the discussion.

Acquiring Fans for your Facebook Page

We have already discussed that when you own a page on Facebook, you invariably become your company's first fan. In addition to this, everybody who visits and likes your page become fans of it too. People can also search for the product and service you endorse, leading to them visiting your page. This helps market your brand and company onto a global platform. When a fan or visitor likes your page, a post is displayed on their own Facebook page. This can be seen by their fans and contacts, thereby increasing your prospects at reaching out to over a million possible clients.

Sharing and Marketing your Facebook Page

To share your page with others and market it to a million Facebook users:

1. Post a message with a link to your Facebook page.
2. Click the button that reads Share Location in the lower left corner of the screen. Facebook allows you to directly send the link via a message to a maximum of 20 friends. You can also post a message with your link on your personal profile. Either way, you are guaranteed to grab attention and get noticed.

Friends receiving your message will get an invite to visit your page and become fans. In addition, you can request they share the link with others and, in the process, create a viral marketing strategy.

Creating a Viral Marketing Strategy with Pages

Building a page does not guarantee visitors—not unless you have an aggressive marketing strategy. Luckily for you, by choosing to launch your business page on a platform such as Facebook, you now enjoy the best marketing strategies to run your page. The same strategy that made Facebook as popular and viral as it is today will run your page from the background.

To market your page, you only have to do what you do best: discuss your brand and products in a way that it gets noticed. Use your passion for the brand and line of business to gather interest and curiosity. The more people are interested, the more they'll keep coming back and the more they will be inclined to become customers. Here are a few ways to market your page:

- Add applications to your page.
  In a world that is run by fancy gadgets and programmed apps, adding apps to your page will help you catch everybody's attention. What's more, with the status updated on your wall and newsfeeds, there is no way you'll go unnoticed. Facebook has a list of apps you can choose from. From SlideShare app to the birthday calendar, Facebook has an app for every occasion.
- Post and share messages and opinions on your page.
  If you're a good writer, blog and write articles that are relevant to your line of work. Alternatively, you can share and post interesting articles and events that are in a social context

relevant to your field. You can also use the What's on your Mind dialogue box to speak your thoughts.

- Comment and help the conversion move further. Sometimes a discussion can get stuck and die down, resulting in minimal activity on your page. Keep energy levels high by helping the conversation move along. So go ahead, keep them talking and interested. Add value to the conversation by pitching in with some insights and information. Show them you are technically equipped for what you do.

Getting Your Fans to Market Pages For You

Your fans are your frontrunners. They are the reason you stay visible and buzzing on the site. It is therefore important that your gather their interest and support to market your page. Here are few ways you can do so:

- Become a fan of your fans' pages. This can create mutual understanding and goodwill between you. This will help you collectively work toward uplifting your brand's visibility and reach.
- Inviting your fans to join discussions by contributing to your wall posts is a great way to make your brand and marketing strategy viral.
- Uploading photos and tagging relevant people seen in the photos is a great way to find your way to their pages and a whole world of potential customers.

- Creating and uploading videos displays your knowledge on a topic. Inviting people to view and rate the video will bring in a lot of traffic to your page.
- Hold an event and market it aggressively on Facebook. Invite fans and friends to the event while offering discounts if they refer and/or bring more people to your event.

To find a page on Facebook:

1. In the Search box, key in the name of the organization, event, product or personality you wish to locate and click Enter
2. You can also click on the Pages tab located at the top of the screen. This will list a broader search.
3. Lastly, you can view pages by their type. To locate a page by its type:

- Click on the Profile link on top of the navigation bar.
- Click on the Info tab.
- Scroll down and click the See all Link.
- Click Browse all Pages.
- Select the page you want to view.

Facebook displays pages based on its popularity and visits. This method will help you list and view pages within a particular category.

Advertising on Facebook

Creating a strong marketing strategy is all about advertising your brand so that it has maximum reach. By advertising your business page on Facebook, you increase your winning stakes by two-fold. Let's look at some important things to consider while building a strong and formidable advertising strategy.

Setting Your Objectives

Identify your goals based on the reach you hope to have. This will help you identify who your target audiences are.

Facebook allows you to place ads under three major categories, namely:

- a traditional text ad – might consist of texts and characters only
- a display ad – can be a combination of text and images
- a unique Facebook engagement ad – can only be ordered through a Facebook advertising representative and requires you to interact with the Facebook's `directly.

Setting Up Your Advertisement

If you are well versed in common interactive-marketing terms, then you should know the importance of a landing page. The landing page shows up as soon as the ad link is clicked. This page acts as the first point of contact for your brand and has a window of a few seconds to hold the attention of the viewer. To create a lasting impression on the viewer, it is important to create a dynamic landing page for your ad that promises to hold the audience's attention long enough to influence a sale.

Creating a Facebook Ad

Whether you are creating a basic text ad or a simple display ad, the steps are fairly simple and easy to follow. Unique ads can only be created by the ad team and are therefore not available at your end.

1. Once you've logged into Facebook and are on the main screen of your page, scroll to the bottom of the screen and click on the link that reads Advertising.
2. Now, click the Ads Manager link to view the Facebook Ads page.
3. Click the button that reads Create an Ad, positioned in the middle left corner of your screen, and design your ad.
4. Choose a suitable objective for your ad campaign.
5. You may choose to design a simple text or a display ad. Pay attention to detail and keep your message simple and effective. While choosing an image for your ad, focus on quality and resolution, so it has maximum impact.
6. Under destination URL, click on the link that reads I Want to Advertise Something I Have on Facebook.
   You will be prompted with a list of events, products and pages you previously endorsed. Choose the right internal destination and write a little about your ad. This will be displayed as the headline for your ad so you need to keep it simple and effective.
7. Once you are satisfied with your headline description, click on Upload an Image and select

the image you want your ad to have. Note that you may choose to ignore this step if you wish to create a text-only ad.

8. Click Publish to make your ad visible

Targeting Audiences for Your Facebook Ad Campaign

1. Select the location in which you want to publish your ad and make it visible. Facebook allows you to target 100 countries while reaching out to 25 countries for a single ad. Note that you can further narrow your targeted locale by specifying the city, state or province in which you wish to publish your ad.
2. Select the age range of your audience. While the minimum age is 13 years and above, there is no upper age limit.
3. Select the gender you want to target. For example, a lipstick brand might target women in particular.
4. Select any keywords you'd like to use to target your audiences.
5. Select your audience's preferred work designations.
6. Select your audience's desired education level .
7. Select a preferred work sector.
8. Select your audience's relationship status.
9. Select your audience's target language.
10. Lastly, select Save All to save the information.

Creating Multiple Ad Campaigns

With Facebook Ads, there is no restriction to the possibilities. That is why they allow you create multiple ad campaigns. With Facebook, you can duplicate an existing ad, edit and make necessary changes to it such that it suits your new requirement. You can also launch multi-faceted ad campaigns.

Here are some of the reasons an advertiser might choose to use multiple ads:

- In order to target different geographical areas based on their demographic tastes and interests. Each place has a culture that influences its tastes and interests. So, while an ad might have worked well in a particular location, it might not necessarily to do so in another. Therefore, by editing and changing ads to address the sensitivities of a new audience, you are saving yourself additional money you might have incurred in creating a new ad campaign altogether. What's more, you retain the relevancies of the campaign and only need to adjust the things that specifically need to be changed.
- Increase the impact and overall effectiveness of your campaign. Using multiple languages for different geographical locations will help you communicate your message in a manner that new audiences understand the best.
- Address any shortcomings of the campaign. Using the first few campaigns to gauge the audience's reactions will allow you to alter your

campaign to better target specific audiences and/or avoid possible predicted problems.

Using Facebook Chatbots

Today, chatbots are much more than just online chatrooms where teenagers practice new words and make new friends. They are an online platform created to simulate conversations with real humans using the power of Artificial Intelligence. Facebook launched a new messaging tool known as Facebook chatbot that allows pages to engage with users, automatically offering sales services and 24/7 support through the messenger.

If you wonder why anyone would need a chatbot, consider all those times when you wasted hours trying to get your questions answered on a customer support line. Those simple queries might have been easily solved with a visit to a FAQ section. Hence, if someone could take this burden from your shoulders and free up your time so that you can focus on other important things, it would be really great. And that's exactly what Facebook chatbot is trying to achieve.

Moreover, solving your queries is not the only thing a chatbot can do for you. It makes recommendations based on users' preferences and previous purchases, such as music albums. Chatbot performs quick data analysis and recommends services or products based on its analysis, establishing a more personalized experience with users.

Chatbots provide well-written, clear, subject-related quick answers, eliminating the endless phone line wait time. The years of hard work put in by experts to enable AI to do real things, in real time, has made a huge difference in our cultural references and the way people are seeing bots today as more than just simple codes written by experts. Today, chatbots expedite and enhance customer experience.

How to use Facebook Chatbot

The first step to using a chatbot is choosing the platform you want to use to create it. Although using Facebook's in-house platform is a perfect option, you might want to explore other platforms, such as Botsify, Chatfuel, etc. for a more simplified and user-friendly experience, particularly if you do not have any programming experience. The good news is that these platforms are absolutely free unless you are planning to do something really complex with them. Once you have decided which platform you will use to create your chatbot, create an account and then connect it to your designated Facebook page.

Once you have the platform on, you can start creating the dialogue that your chatbot will use to engage with users. Come up with an interesting welcome message that goes well with your business. Think of a suitable tone, and see if the answers you provide your users can include images, videos, forms or just text. Decide the next steps for the visitor once they have provided the information to the chatbot. An important thing here is to test everything you do before going live.

Chatbots are really valuable, and part of this is due to their flexibility. Let's look at some Facebook chatbots, all of which can uniquely benefit your business.

Chatbots That Provide Personalized Content Experience

There are certain chatbots created to focus only on content, with a goal of serving as extensions of content market strategy. They are known to nurture relationships with users and deliver personalized content experiences so that users receive immediate value without doing real work at their end. Consider an example. A chatbot known as Whole Foods helps its users find recipes. When they enter keywords like "desserts," the chatbot takes them through a series of personalized questions based on their query. Once the users answer the queries, the chatbot displays the results and users can view a recipe by simply tapping on one. The chatbot will then take the users to a recipe on its website. It's a great way to drive traffic to your website from social media without making it feel like spam. You're helping your customers find the content they are looking for and generating traffic in exchange.

While creating the design for a content-focused chatbot for your audience, keep in mind the following:

- Make sure the underlying website is mobile responsive.
- Treat it as a content marketing platform. Your primary goal for designing the chatbot shouldn't be to sell but to drive traffic to your website with the help of the content.
- Inform your audience how and where they can contact you.

- Add browsing options, if possible. This will make it easy for your audience to look for the content they are searching for.

Chatbots That Address Customer Queries

One common application for chatbots is addressing customer service questions that are commonly asked. You just need to program it to be able to handle these cases. Consider the Domino's Pizza chatbot as an example to understand this scenario. It helps customers to place an order and track it using a simple and effective Track Order tool. Customers commonly ask questions like when their order will get delivered or how much time will it take. Teaching your chatbot to handle such important but simple queries allows you to focus on other more pressing business matters.

When designing a customer-service-centric chatbot, always remember to:

- Ensure customers can reach out to a live customer service agent when needed.
- Let the users know they are dealing with an automated response system. Tricking your users into believing that they are dealing with real agents isn't a good idea.
- Direct your customers to an agent via your website if any of their personal details need to be verified. Personal information is sensitive, and such data shouldn't be exchanged on social media channels.

Chatbots That Can Streamline Product Purchases

Though chatbots can't replace talented salespeople, they can still be efficiently designed to streamline your product purchases and offer products your customers have been looking for, driving more sales and enhancing your profit margin. Let's look at a chatbot that is designed for buying flowers online. Once the customer fills in details, such as name, phone number, delivery address and so on, the chatbot asks the customer to select the category of products he/she wants to purchase. After the customer selects the category, the chatbot displays the relevant products. Customers can then select a product and enter the delivery details. The chatbot then asks the customer to input billing information so that a payment can be made.

When designing a chatbot to help you streamline your purchases, you must remember to:

- Ensure the chatbot answers customers' FAQs as this helps boost sales.
- Use a builder tool that can accept payments through safe and secured services, such as PayPal. This added function can drive more sales.
- Ask your customers if they need anything other than the selected product before they enter their billing information.

Chatbots That Can Build Connections Via Entertainment

If your goal is to build or nurture relationships with clients, chatbot can be built in a way such that customers can choose to receive news, facts, games, updates and entertaining content.

For example – Trivia Blast is a chatbot that has been designed with the aim to entertain its users. Once the users download and connect with this chatbot, the tool sends them various suggestions and newsfeeds on a regular basis to keep them engaged. Users can then sort the content and games and select what they are interested in. There are several other options also available to the user with these chatbots, such as challenging another friend to play a game or inviting them to read a blog.

When designing a chatbot that can entertain clients, you must keep the following in mind:

- Ensure all content can be accessed on mobile devices.
- Reach out to customers periodically, asking them if they would like to receive new content, news feeds, suggestions, etc.
- Utilize the power of visual media in addition to text.

Chatbots That Can Offer Specialized Services

Businesses using apps for their specific services are quite common on the market these days, but you can go one step further and create a chatbot for your business.

One of the best examples of this kind of chatbot is Remit Radar, whose chatbot offers services to send money, request exchange rates, pay for international purchases and so on. All these operations are streamlined and easy.

When building a chatbot to perform specialized services, remember the following:

- Offer clickable, preset menus to navigate your automated services to make the entire process easy and clear.
- Test and verify your services on various kinds of devices before you go live.
- Refer users to relevant places on your website if they ask something your chatbot can't handle.

Using Instagram to Build Your Brand

When anyone talks about using social media platforms to promote a business, most businesspeople think about Facebook and LinkedIn. They assume Instagram is only for those who like to share pictures or promote their fashion/travel sites. This is because these food lovers, fashionistas and travel junkies constantly share updates about what they just had, what they are wearing, where they are, etc., in an attempt to drive traffic to their sites. But Instagram is for everyone, and influencers and brands are now utilizing this platform in some of the most creative ways to boost their sales and get reviews for their products and services. With Instagram, you can grow your following, engage them, build a strong relationship with your target audience, sell your products and drive traffic to your website. Instagram is a visual social media marketing tool.

Therefore, if you want to promote your private label, start by showing off on Instagram right away.

Use Instagram to:

- Increase your brand awareness by targeting mass audiences.
- Market your business.
- Drive traffic to your site.

The influential marketers and businessmen who have been using this platform for their specific needs love it due to these certain reasons:

1. **The Quality of Images:** Images that are available on Instagram are visually attractive and give the users an opportunity to provide their clients/audience with the best.
2. **Instant:** With Instagram, you can build an immediate target audience for your product or business by posting content as well as images.
3. **Easy and Fun:** All you need to do is snap, edit, add a caption and hashtag. Then start sharing the images and playing around with the features.
4. **Build your Identity:** Users share content and images to define who they are and what they do. This helps them let their audience know what their beliefs and values are, which in turn helps the audience to uniquely identify them.

With all that in mind, promote your private label following these simple steps:

1. **Create an Account**

Before you create an account, you have to think about your brand name and how you would like to market it. For example, let's say you are trying to sell women's apparel. Would you like to market your brand name, or do you want to personally connect with your customers? If you want to market your brand and only advertise your company's name, then you should create an account with the company's name as the user ID and put up the company's logo as the display picture.

On the other hand, if you want to connect with your customers, you can create an account using your name. If you're selling apparel, you might want to make it interesting by modeling the clothes yourself. This will not only showcase the clothes, but will also appeal to users, helping them feel a personal connection with you. You can also always make your brand known by putting up your company's logo as the display picture.

Whether you are creating an account in your name or your company's, you have the option of mentioning your brand website on your profile page. The website link will appear on your Instagram page, and when users click on the link, it will redirect them to your website. If you don't have a website, you can put up a link to your blog so that users can get to know more about you. This is one opportunity you have to lead clicks onto your site, so don't miss using it.

When you are creating an account, choose a username that is relevant to your brand. For example, if you are selling accessories and your company's name is GenX Accessories, choosing a username like genx.accessories or genx_accessories will be helpful. Don't choose a username that has nothing to do with your brand because people will not remember it and each time they see your posts, they won't be reminded of your brand. Keep it interesting and light, and at the same time, it should sound "salesy." Every single time you upload a post, your customers have to know who you are and what you do. Your brand name should keep hitting their minds until it becomes akin to a mantra.

As far as the display picture goes, you can play around with it a bit, but going with your company's logo is the safest bet.

Ensure that your bio is interesting and informative as, before anyone hits your post, they have to click through to your bio; it is going to be the last thing your visitors see before deciding to follow you. So win their hearts and convince them of the content and value you will add to their feeds!

2. Take Good Quality Images

Remember that Instagram users know the different kinds of people that put up their pictures on the site every day. It's important that you create a certain image for yourself so that you come across as fun-loving yet serious about your business. Remember, you are not a teenager who is posting random things on Instagram. You are a brand owner, and you are there to make your brand popular. Therefore, stick mainly to brand-oriented images.

If you want to make people sit up and take notice of your images, invest in a good camera phone. You can take pictures with your digital camera and then transfer

238

the photographs to your phone, but that will be tiresome. Instagram has a specific image size, so pictures taken by other cameras might get cropped while uploading. It's better to buy a smartphone that has a good HD camera so that you can quickly upload excellent quality images and videos.

Let's assume that you specialize in selling cupcakes and own a small bakery. You can upload images of the different types of cupcakes that you sell. Take long and close shots of all the cupcakes. Make sure that they have been shot from top and side angles. Remember that Instagram doesn't limit the number of images you can upload in a day. So, start uploading as many pictures as you can. Use a clever caption and let your customers know the cupcake flavors. Make your captions interesting and attractive. For example, instead of just writing Red Velvet Cupcake, you can write something like "Delicious Red Velvet Cupcake with a fresh cream cheese frosting." This will instantly raise the interests of users. When you are taking pictures, make sure that the background is interesting. For example, you can add in a ribbon or some cute cutlery. Additionally, you can also put a candle on the cupcake indicating that people can buy your product for birthdays and parties.

Regarding pictures, you should know that apart from selling your product, you can also use photographs to give customers an insight into your business. You don't have to keep promoting your product all the time. Bring some variety to your posts so that users are not bored. Using the cupcake example, you can take a selfie with your product and upload it. Or, you can shoot a short

15-second video that shows your kitchen and all the items that go into making the cupcakes. You can also post a quick recipe telling users how to make easy chocolate or vanilla cupcakes at home. Take a picture of your staff and let people know about the day-to-day activities happening in your kitchen. This will pique the interest of users, and they will connect with you personally, and in the process, your brand will get promoted.

3. Use as Many Hashtags as You Can

One of the most effective and simple ways to become popular on Instagram and reach out to millions of people is through the use of hashtags.

Everything in this world is changing fast, and so are Instagram feeds. With this changing environment, all posts are short-lived, and your content gets buried quickly. So, lump your content together into groups or communities by tagging them with a hashtag which will always be discoverable. Brainstorm and come up with keywords or phrases that can uniquely define your brand or product. See what's trending and use related hashtags.

You can use as many hashtags as you want. Remember to use your brand name with them. This way people will come to know about your brand, and when they click on the hashtags, they will see all your products on the same page. For example, let's assume you are selling coffee and your brand is known as Star Coffee. When you are using hashtags, use them profusely. Use hashtags like #starcoffee, #starcoffecappucino, #starcoffeecalifornia, etc. This will widen the reach of your post, and more users will come to know about your brand.

Also remember to use general hashtags like #coffee, #latte, #expresso, because people will not know about your brand when they are searching for coffee. They will use general hashtags, and if you don't have them in your image, they will not show up in others' feeds. Therefore, it is important to use as many relevant hashtags as you can. Follow the trends used by Instagram. It takes a few seconds for a trend to go viral on Instagram. For example, the hashtag #HalloweenFood may take only a couple of minutes to become popular on October 31st. Keep an eye out for such trends and use them as hashtags for your pictures.

You should also check out the hashtags that are most widely used. For example, hashtags like #instafood, #instaphotography, #instapic, etc. are used by people for almost all their photographs. Look out for such hashtags and use them in all your photographs. Remember that the more hashtags you use, the more popular your images will be.

4. Get Followers

Every Instagram user's greatest desire is to accrue a large number of followers. That applies to you as a business person as well. If you want people to take your business seriously, you have to make sure that people first follow you and then stay loyal. Here are a few tips for how to achieve this:

Make it a point to always shoot good images – Don't take your users lightly. For example, if you own a huge company and you want to promote your brand as the best online store for buying clothes, shoes and accessories, you have to do some hard work. When you are doing photo shoots for your online store, take some images for Instagram. Remember that Instagram users have a liking for quirky images so you can shoot some images where the background is unusual. For example, if you are shooting pictures for apparel and your models are working out of a studio, make an arrangement for an outdoor shoot.

You can take some pictures on the beach, in a garden or in a popular restaurant. This will bring some variety to your pictures. If you keep posting images of your models standing in front of a white background, people will lose interest no matter how good your products are. If someone is looking for a nice outfit, they also like to see the kind of mood and setting that will go well with a suit or a dress. People like to imagine themselves in a certain location wearing a newly-purchased garment. Use that to your advantage and make your posts interesting and attractive. This way you will gain a loyal number of followers who are curious to know what you are going to post next.

Always keep a surprise in store for your users – Give them a hint about what you are going to post next. For example, if you are going to do a photo shoot near the seaside, let them know about it. You can use captions like "Watch out for our next post that will give you a taste of the sea, salt and style." Readers want something new every time, and if you can keep them interested, they will start following you.

Ask for users' opinions when you are posting images – Ask them if they like the images and what would they like to see next. Take their opinions seriously and make sure that you live up to your promises. People appreciate individuals who take their opinions seriously. Reply to their comments and let them know that you appreciate their compliments and suggestions. A little communication with your users will go a long way in building a rapport with them. This will ensure that your followers stay loyal and don't unfollow you.

Comment on people's posts – Watch for a variety of images on Instagram and keep commenting on people's posts. Compliment them and ask them to look at your profile. Remember that nobody is looking for your brand unless you make an effort to make it popular. Keep commenting and complimenting, and you are sure to get a good number of followers. However, don't keep commenting the same thing over and over again. Additionally, you should follow a few people to show that you are really interested in them, and they will likely follow you in return.

5. Keep Your Followers Engaged

Now that you have earned your share of followers, you need to make sure that they stick around. Remember that it's easy to lose followers but very tough to gain them. You must make it a habit to upload a minimum of five posts every day. Ideally, you should upload as many as you can, but if you are too tied up with other work, upload at least five images. Remember that your followers have many other posts to concentrate on, and if you don't make your presence felt, you will soon be off their radar. Unless you show up on their feed regularly, nobody is going to think of you. Therefore, it is very important that you maintain consistency on Instagram.

You can also keep your followers engaged by throwing contests for them. It makes your brand popular and earns you more followers. For example, if you are selling handbags, you can hold a contest where you ask people to tag your brand on all their handbag-related posts. You can tell them that the best post will win an exclusive bag from your brand. This will definitely raise interests among users, and they will tag you on their posts. When they are tagging you, their followers are also getting to know about you. As a result, your brand is being promoted just through a simple contest.

Make sure the contest duration is not too long. Ideally, you should announce the winner within a week. To make them popular on your Instagram profile, post their winning picture and tell them how much you like it. Also tell your other users that you would love to host more such contests and that everyone has an equal chance of winning. Send the winner their prize with a nice congratulatory note. This is a good investment as the winner will tell their friends and family about it and your brand will become popular through word-of-mouth publicity.

Decide what you want to give to your audience. If you don't have the budget to give out prizes, just repost the name of the winner and tell your followers how much you liked the winning post. People love fame, and if you can help them become famous, that is all they will need. Feature their posts in your Instagram account and ask users to follow them. Repeat this exercise for a number of users and you will become gain a following in no time at all. Once you have collected a huge number of followers, you can lower the number of contests and make your posts more brand-oriented.

Remember that engaging with your followers is one of the best, easiest and cheapest ways of gaining followers and popularity for your brand. You just have to come up with creative ideas and good quality pictures.

6. Get a Celebrity to Endorse Your Brand

Getting a celebrity to endorse your brand will definitely devour a chunk of your budget. On the plus side, you will get a lot of followers instantly, and the sale of your products will increase. When you have a celebrity endorse your brand, you can use the same picture or video on a number of social media platforms.

Also use some pictures from those shoots on your Instagram account. Use relevant hashtags and request that the celebrity follow your account. People keep checking their favorite celebrities' profiles, and they usually have a tendency to follow similar brands. For example, if your brand is being followed by a very popular celebrity and they post a picture with your brand, there is no doubt that you will gain instant popularity. Imagine a popular Hollywood actress sporting a pair of shoes from your brand. Suddenly, people will want to know everything about your brand and your company and this will go a long way to ensuring your success.

However, you don't necessarily have to burn a hole in your pocket to launch your brand on Instagram. If you know someone who is known for their fashion sense and has a good number of followers, you can ask them to endorse your brand. Just ask them to either repost your images on their account or pose for your brand.

Nowadays, there are many people who have taken to Instagram to promote themselves as fashion bloggers. If you are selling apparel and accessories, you can contact them and ask them to pose with some of your products and tag your brand in all their posts. Some of these bloggers have a huge following, and people usually look up to them when it comes fashion. So, getting some posts done by them will give you good publicity.

There are also users who are passionate about a number of subjects like photography, food, biking, nature and art. No matter what your brand is, you will be able to find someone who can promote it through their profile. People take foodies and photographers seriously, and if they promote your brand, the chances are that your sales will grow exponentially.

7. Create a Blog and Promote it on Instagram

There are many users who use a single picture to promote their brand. How? Let's assume that you are selling kitchen equipment. No one is interested in knowing about a boring piece of equipment, but you can hold an audience's interest if you can tell them how they can use a specific item to make their favorite dishes. For example, if you have launched some baking equipment, post a picture on Instagram and provide a link to your blog in the caption section.

You can easily create a blog account through Google or Wordpress. Write a recipe on how to bake delicious cakes and mention how people can use your equipment to make their cakes look professional and taste like heaven. Remember that nowadays a lot of activities happen online because people use their smartphones and tablets to read articles on the Internet. While your kitchen equipment may look uninteresting on its own, people will realize its importance once they read your blog, hear your stories and see your pictures.

Similarly, you can post similar blogs on fashion, food, jewelry, etc. If you think that you can't dedicate enough time to writing such blog posts, remember that there are many freelancers out there who are willing to do it for you at a low price. You can tell them about your requirements, and they will write an article for you. This way you will be able to connect your users to your brand, and your popularity will not just be limited to Instagram.

8. Use Instagram Ads Feature

Recently, Instagram introduced an ads feature where your brand's ad will appear on users' feeds. You can pay Instagram to promote your brand, and they will advertise it for you. For example, if you are selling hair care products, your ad will appear on the feeds of users who are interested in beauty and hair-related posts. They will see it in their feed just like a normal post, but when they tap on it, it will direct them to your website, where they can buy the product. This is an easy way of getting your brand promoted, albeit a bit expensive. However, if you have set aside a big budget for marketing and promoting your brand, you can easily buy ad space from Instagram.

Remember, Instagram offers users the flexibility of not seeing your ad if they don't find it relevant or interesting. They can easily choose to hide it from their feed. To stop that from happening, you should post ads that are fun and engaging. You don't have to put your product in their face all the time. Come up with creative and funny ad ideas so that users don't delete you from their feed. Take cues from some popular brands and see how they entertain their consumers. Post a beautiful picture or make an interesting video and always encourage users to go to your website for more information. This way your brand will stay in the minds of users for a long time.

Using the ideas in this chapter, you can measure your success in order to continue growing and make sure you do not let your Instagram plateau. Keep it going, keep attracting and engaging your existing and new customers. The most effective way to continue optimizing this social media platform to maintain growth is to analyze your success from time to time. Research your audience; see what's working and what's not. Pay attention to some of the top metrics to see where you were and where you are today.

Track your Reciprocity: You can keep a check on your reciprocity to find your loyal customers. Reciprocity will show you which of your visitors engage and show interest in your brand the most, who are the ones to like your product the most, who is tagging you and your brand the most and so on. If you want to continue appealing to these important audiences and earn more likes/shares from them, it is important that you recognize them. Knowing and giving them a shout-out will improve your chances of success and strengthen the relationship with these customers.

Track your Density: You can track density to optimize your Instagram postings. This helps you understand when and what time of the day your followers engage most often with your posts. According to studies and research, the best time to post on Instagram is between 6 p.m. and 7 p.m. on Mondays. Although your specific followers might have different schedules, this is a sweet spot according to experts. Why track density? This is because knowing what time your audience is active will help you optimize your shares and likes. Another important thing to note is that you should post on a consistent schedule. It is always good to remain active on your follower's trends consistently. When your followers know you post at a specific time, they will know when to expect to see a post from you. Be active on their feeds, but at the same time, do not overcrowd them. Analyze your density statistics to see the ideal time and schedule and post only one or two posts during that slot.

Instagram Stories

Another feature offered by Instagram is Instagram Stories, which lets its users post videos and images that last for 24 hours. The stories are very similar to Snapchat Stories, which was introduced in 2013. In your Instagram Story, you can share content that doesn't need to be viewed after 24 hours. It appears at the top of the feeds, in a bar and when there is something new to show to the world, your profile pic will have a colorful ring around it. If someone wants to view your story, he or she can just tap on your profile pic and the content will play on their screen in chronological order.

Stories can be created simply. Just tap on the plus button that appears at the top left corner of the screen and record your story. You can add images or a video and use a range of filters too.

Instagram stories are an effective means to keep your loyal customers or followers engaged while leaving your content open for new site visitors to view. Though the reality is that the content is erased in 24 hours, it is a means to keep the audience addicted and engaged. The ephemerality of the stories adds authenticity to the content, and this is another reason it helps you get more traffic to your site.

Another positive side of this ephemeral content is that since the stories are temporary in nature, you can repost this content on other channels without worrying about the consistency you have set across the various social channels for your business.

Here are a few tips to keep in mind while creating stories on Instagram:

- Always use the right hashtags at the right places, for the right reasons. Generally, hashtags increase the exposure of your content, and they are likely to take your audience away from the main content. Therefore, use hashtags only if they are related to your post and brand.

- Use location tags in your stories as they will help you be discovered in various locations. Tagging your location in a story when relevant is a good way to make it visible to people who might be checking posts for that location.
- Use Instagram Live to add value to your Instagram Stories.

Instagram Ads

Instagram is not just for travel junkies or fashionistas; it has something to offer to everyone including businesses of all sizes and types. But as more brands and businesses are becoming active on Instagram, the environment is becoming more competitive, making survival difficult. Even so, Instagram is opening new doors for its users. One such initiative taken by Instagram has been introducing Instagram Ads. After the success of Facebook Ads, marketers were looking for another platform where they could reach out to specific segments of users. With millions of people using Instagram day and night, Instagram Ads have become the next enticing tool for these marketers and businessmen.

Instagram Ads offer an incredibly powerful and easy-to-use tool to reach a target audience. Here are certain ways to create and manage your ads on this platform:

- Facebook Ads Manager
- Within the Instagram App

- Power Editor
- Instagram Partners
- Facebook Marketing API

Using Facebook Ads Manager

There is no denying that the advertising platform Facebook offers its users is comprehensive and easy to use. So, exploit it to create your Instagram Ads by following these steps:

1. Choose your marketing objective.
2. Select a compelling name for your campaign.
3. Define your budget, ad placement, audience and schedule.
4. Create a new ad or use an existing post.

Navigate to the Facebook Ads Manager by clicking the drop-down menu on the Facebook page and select Manage Ads. Click on Create Ad and get started.

Next, select your marketing objective. While Facebook offers 11 objectives to create ads on its platform, only eight can be used to create Instagram Ads: Traffic, Reach, Brand Awareness, Conversions, App Installs, Video Views, Engagement and Lead Generation. Based on your requirements, select one of these marketing objectives. While some of these options are straightforward, others might involve one or two simple additional steps. For instance, if your marketing objective is Reach, after entering your campaign name, you will be asked to choose a Facebook page to link to this campaign. In the case of Traffic, you will be asked to choose the destination where you wish to drive your traffic. It could be either your mobile or desktop app or the website. So, add information for these additional steps whenever required.

Now, define your budget, ad placement, audience and schedule.

Audience – you can define your target audience based on factors, such as location, gender, age, interests, demographics, languages, behaviors, etc. You can also define your own set based on who has interacted with you the most and tag it as your Custom Audience. You can even create a Lookalike Audience just the way you did in the case of a Facebook ad. Once you select the criteria, you will be shown information about your target audience based on the potential reach, how broad or specific they are, your targeting criteria and daily estimated reach.

Ad Placement – This is a very important step and the effectiveness of your ads depends a lot on where they are placed. By default, your Ads Manager selects the placement for ads on both Facebook and Instagram. If you are looking at only Instagram Ads, for now, select Edit Placements and then deselect Facebook from the list of platforms. Using the advanced options, you can also specify the operating systems and mobile devices on which you want your ads to be available.

Budget – Think about how much you want to spend on these ads it and set your budget accordingly. You can either set a daily budget or lifetime. While the daily budget is the average amount that you spend on your Instagram Ads each day, your lifetime budget is what you spend on them over the lifetime of the ad.

Schedule – You can schedule your ads by either letting them run continuously or setting a start/end date and time.

To create your ads, choose a format and get started. Instagram offers its users six ad formats, out of which four are for Feed Ads (Carousel, Single Video, Single Image and Slideshow) and two for Stories Ads (Single Image and Single Video).

Carousel ads have two or more scrollable videos or images. To create an ad of this type, connect to your Instagram account and create cards for your ad. The maximum limit is ten cards for a single carousel. To create a card, simply upload a video, image or slideshow and enter the headlines. Include the destination URL and select the most suitable call-to-action option.

Single Image ads have just one image, and if you decide to go with this format, you can have up to six ads with one image per ad. Fill in all the required details, and you are good to go.

Similarly, you can create the other types of ads as well.

Using Instagram App To Create The Ads

If you do not want to use Facebook Ads Manager to create your marketing ads, you can choose to go with Instagram App to promote an existing Instagram post or a new one.

1. Select what you want to promote. Select the existing post and click on the Promote button.

2. Select an ad objective. Instagram offers you two options—visit your website and Call/Visit your business.
3. Set your audience, budget, action and duration. Depending on the ad objective you have selected, decide your action item, enter your destination link and other details, such as address and phone number.

Using Pinterest to Build your Brand

In addition to Instagram and Facebook, another social media platform for you to explore is Pinterest. Today, Pinterest is a hot piece of property, especially for marketing purposes. But again, it's not just for food lovers and travel bloggers; Pinterest's the real forte is the features it offers you to market your brand on one of the most popular platforms. It allows its users to create and share content and visuals by pinning videos and images to collages created on various topics.

Every pin you create is linked to the source of the video or image, be it an article, blog post or a website that provides more details about that pin. When you share someone else's pin, you repin. If you are repining from somewhere, mention why you think this will be beneficial content for your customers. Never forget to mention your brand name and site URL in your caption. Pins can be grouped together by topic onto pinboards.

Understand that Pinterest for business marketing is different from Pinterest for personal use. The business account taps into added perks for marketing potency based on your goals, and you will receive:

- Enhanced traffic
- Increased sales
- Enhanced brand awareness
- Improved engagement with potential customers
- Buzz around your business.

Maximize Your Content

Pinterest hasn't ceased growing and attracting visitors over the years, and this makes it a worthwhile distributing platform. Follow these marketing tactics to maximize your Pinterest results:

- **Keep your board title short and memorable** – Fun, eye-catching titles tend to attract more visitors to your board. However, don't name your board something that will be hard to find. Find a way to incorporate your business name and keywords into your board title without sounding too formal. Two to five-word titles are optimum.

- **Caption pins concisely** – Make sure you have explained each pin and provided the required context. Wherever possible, incorporate your board category in the description. Use words effectively so that they aid in searchability. Most descriptions of pins are usually four to fourteen words.

- **Widen the conversation while keeping it focused** – Using hashtags often expand the conversation on social media. Not a lot of businesses are using hashtags on Pinterest yet, but it is a sound strategy nonetheless.

- **Engage with your audience** – However, don't overdo it. As on Twitter, you can use the @ sign to engage with a participant.

- **Follow your customers** – but don't feel obligated to do so. Businesses tend to not follow customers. However, if your business works on audience participation, you might be better off following a few customers.

- **Think visually** – Even if your product isn't a visual one, try to think of ways to add images (relevant ones) to add more value to your Pinterest boards.

- **People are attracted to people, not robots** – You could have a board devoted to staff members and include headshots with bios or pins of exhibits you have had. People tend to trust your business more if they can see that you are as human as they are.

- **Infographic** – Yes, we've mentioned this before, but it is certainly one of the most viewed categories on Pinterest. If you write blog posts that explain concepts of how-tos, you can include an image or infographic to increase the visual appeal. Make sure they're easy to read and provide relevant information to your target demographic.

- **Add the Pin It button to your blog posts** – This will remind your readers to share the post with their Pinterest followers.

- **Pin your content with pictures of your products** – Possibilities include eBooks or books from your website. Make sure the cover is aesthetically appealing and that you provide all the relevant information, such as where to purchase the item and how it will help your customers.

- **Pin various types of media** – You can even pin videos, webinars and audio tracks like podcasts if they're relevant to your niche.

- **Don't fill your board with only your content** – People appreciate it when you share others' content. Repinning will garner more interest from your followers, and they'll be more open to your original content.

- **Create shared boards where others can contribute** – This increases your chances of being viewed. You can create a board where your customers can contribute by showing ways they're using your product, for example. The advantage of this is that each contributor's follower count might become interested in your board, so you will reach a greater number of people.

- **Post pins in a timely fashion** – If you have a product that will be of good use during Christmas, then start pinning in October so that it provides enough time for the pin to circulate and have increased visibility.

- **Pin often, but control your content** – Make sure you are pinning often enough to stay in the minds of your followers, but don't flood or spam your followers' pages.

In order to maximize your Pinterest results, enhance your pins with relevant and findable content.

What to Pin

When the business value of a social media network doesn't seem clear, it can be quite daunting to begin. However, Pinterest isn't just a place to pin your products. Business owners often underestimate the power of this site or are simply unsure about what to pin.

In order to successfully use Pinterest for your business, you will have to look beyond pins that showcase your product. For example, if your business sells window blinds, a board full of images of blinds will probably not be all that interesting to your audience. However, you might pin images that show your product in action, such as a particular kind of window treatment that works well with the rest of the décor in the room, or which has creative styling. These images will be more striking and capture potential customers' attention. It might even be enough incentive for people to repin a few of those images, thus potentially widening your customer base.

You don't have to have a physical product in order to make the most of this site. Any business can be made visually interesting to your target audience. You only need helpful content that offers solutions to people's problems. It can be the services you offer or the core values of your business.

If you own a retail shop, you don't necessarily have to only pin items that you sell. The content you pin needs to reflect the essence of your business. You can include items you currently have or have had in the past, or even similar items that you'd like to have one day in your shop. This will help attract the kind of customer that is interested in what you offer in your shop and inspire them to buy items at your business.

You can use Pinterest for your business even if you don't have an e-commerce site, uploading images of your product directly from your desktop to create a pin. However, don't forget to make it clear to your potential customers how they can buy items from your business. Include a link to your blog or add contact information in the description of the profile as well as your pins.

You can use Pinterest to establish yourself or your brand as an expert in your field. By pinning content from your website, blog and digital assets from your site, you can provide quality information to your followers.

Your audience might be interested in tips and tricks that are related to your industry, and you can create infographics even if your business doesn't have any visual assets. Simply owning a blog opens up a huge area of content for your pins.

Remember that any business can be visual if handled the right way. If you are an accountant, for example, you can pin interesting statistics, infographics about budgeting or tips on how to manage money, etc. You can even create images of your customer testimonials and pin them.

Behind-the-scenes photos of your business can also be interesting to your audience. If you sell handicrafts, for example, your customers might be interested in knowing where the material comes from and how it is turned into the products that you sell. If your products are seasonal, you might be able to pin other content that's relevant to the holiday too. For example, if you sell Christmas-themed mugs, also pin a recipe for a holiday-themed drink that your customers can enjoy along with your product.

Remember, all of this works toward driving traffic and sales toward your business. Establish your goals before you start, and you might be able to increase brand awareness too.

Pay attention to the feedback and stay in your customers' good books.

Increasing Your Social Reach

We have already established that Pinterest is an excellent social media tool to market your product, by getting traffic to your website and business. However, don't forget that forging valuable relationships of trust and respect with your audience is just as important as using the social network as a marketing tool.

There are quite a few things you can do to increase your social reach on Pinterest and gain more referral traffic for your blog, website and business.

- **Add buttons to your blog and website** – These include the Pin It buttons on your blog posts and the 'Follow' buttons on your website. If you want to improve your reach and visibility on the site, you have to make it simple for your users to be able to pin images. People tend to avoid going out of their way just to share content, so if you make it easier for them to access, you will have greater chances of expanding your viewership. The more straightforward it is to access your content, the better results you can expect.

- **Use the browser extension available for Pinterest** – A Pin It button on your browser toolbar makes it easy to pin images from any site, though not everyone uses this. Making your images shareable with just one click will give you better chances. There are a few plug ins for sites like Wordpress to manage your images and to make them Pinterest-friendly.

- **Try to embed pins below your blog posts and see if they work for you** – It's easy to create your own embedded pin. It's just a matter of copying some relevant codes. This is a kind of call-to-action that encourages readers to share your content. But make sure that it doesn't detract from the main goal of your post. For example, if your post is about email subscription lists, your call-to-action should focus on that rather than getting caught up in sharing the posts on social media.

- **Use group boards, containing multiple contributors** – They are a great way to increase your reach. They work just like regular Pinterest boards. However, for each contributor, the pins will be visible to the followers of their boards. This may cause more people to add pins, and you'll have a chance to get more repins, followers and traffic. Creating your own group board is easy, and you can invite other Pinterest users to post on it.

- **Cross-promote on other social media networks** – A good way to get your pins seen is to tweet about your product or share it on Facebook, especially if you already have a healthy follower count on other social media.

- **Share eye-catching content** – Since Pinterest is a visually-driven site, it makes sense that you will need to create aesthetically appealing images for your pins. They are more likely to be shared. Unique images tend to gain more interest. You don't have to be an excellent or trained designer to make these eye-catching images; you can simply use tools that are freely available over the Internet to create content.

Keep the Pinterest image guidelines in mind when creating pictures. Canva is one such free tool that makes it extremely easy for you to create an image. It allows you to choose the default size, which is great because you can then create a high-quality image for your pin. It also has layouts that have been pre-designed to look stunning. You can, of course, customize them to suit your needs using an abundance of available icons, backgrounds and fonts.

Increase Lead Generation

You must know by now that social media can be very effective for lead generation. Studies have shown that shoppers who use Pinterest spend significantly more than the average shopper who isn't a Pinterest user. What this means is that there are a lot of potential leads just waiting to be converted to sales.

Pinterest has proven itself to be a brilliant platform for marketers, brands and businesses. This is because they acknowledge that a presence on Pinterest translates into more sales than their presence on other social media sites. Some ways you can boost lead generation on this site include:

- **Optimize your profile page** – As with any other social network, your profile page provides your audience with the first impression of your business. It is important to remember to keep your personal and professional account separate. Your brand's page should be focused on your business, not your personal interests. Your brand name should be clear and its description concise. In order to optimize your profile and boost visibility on Pinterest, use top keywords that are relevant to your business in your captions and board titles.

- **Pin informative content** – Make sure it will catch the interest of your followers. Attractive pictures drive this website, and if you want your images to go viral on this site, you need to make sure that your pins are easy to understand, helpful and aesthetically pleasing. If you don't add a caption or descriptor to your pin, it can be quite hard to find, which will result in fewer views. Be diligent in adding relevant information to the description. Infographics attract more clicks and repins.

- **Make your pins search-friendly** – Do this by optimizing your images. Since this social network is all about sharing and collecting, driving SEO traffic is easy if you know how. Use targeted keywords to create your board titles and add keywords to your descriptions of the pins. Try to use phrases and words that are not only relevant to your business but also words that your customers are searching for. Use descriptive words as well as the product name so it will rank higher in SEO.

- **Create original content** – People are attracted to unique content on all social media networks. Therefore, you can increase your follower count by pinning fresh and interesting content. If you pin often enough, you have a chance of being featured on Pinterest

Recommendation. This will drive even more leads to your page.

Each time a pin is repinned, Pinterest automatically creates a backlink to the source page. Avoid posting only images of your product or service because if you want your users to interact and engage with your business, it is best not to bombard them with self-promotional images. Know the choices and preferences of your target demographic.

- **Build an audience first** – Social media platforms are only tools, and the aim is to build a community around your brand that paints your business in a positive light. In order to generate leads, build and respect your audience. Be consistent and share interesting and useful content.

- **Run contests** – Giving away something for free is always a great way to catch the attention of your followers. However, before you run any contests, check Pinterest's guidelines and terms of use and follow them carefully. Generate interest in the product you want to give away by sharing images of how it can be used. You will reach a wider audience that will hopefully stay with you even after the contest or giveaway has ended.

- **Follow people who are highly influential** – Engage with them in order to build your community. Chances are, their followers will become your followers too.

Organizing Contests and Free Offers

Since about 80 percent of the pins on Pinterest are just repins, it is a great site to drive engagement, which can be increased to higher levels by running contests. Well-organized contests and free offers can have a very positive impact on your brand and business.

If you manage your Pinterest account effectively, it can help you generate leads, promote participation, gain followers and a lot of other benefits. However, if you don't run your account well, it could also have a negative impact on your brand, and your time and effort will then have been wasted.

The following tips can help you efficiently run a Pinterest contest, with positive results:

- First, read the Terms of Service. As on any social media platform, your account can be suspended if you fail to follow these. However, Pinterest's contest rules are quite lenient. There is a list of do's and don'ts that are easy to understand and follow.
- Set a goal before you start. You can't simply go blundering in blindly and hope that it will result in some leads and follows. You need to organize a contest that is targeted toward achieving the goal you have set for yourself. If your aim is to generate more leads, make sure you collect them by asking people to sign up using their email address. If your aim is to drive more traffic to your website, make sure people either pin

something from your website or share your pins that have links leading back to your site.

- Creating a landing page is a very important part of holding a contest on Pinterest. This is where your audience will be directed in order to get more details about the contest. It is a good idea to have another pinnable image on your landing page. It could also contain instructions on how to take part in the contest and what people will win if they sign up, register or fill out a form.

  A sign-up form is a good way to get your audience enrolled in the contest, as you can't get people to enroll simply with a pin, board or comment. The form can also help you collect leads as well as build a list through which you can later build good relationships. This will all lead to an audience to which you can market your goods at a later date. Free giveaways always encourage more sign-ups. Don't put any unnecessary information on the landing page; the aim is to get more people to sign up. Use simple designs and eye-catching images.

- Make sure you keep the contest easy and fun for everyone involved, not to mention, inexpensive. After signing up, people shouldn't need to do more than make a few pins and repins. If they have to do something complicated that takes a lot of time, most people will not bother with it. Not everyone will be willing to spend money to win a prize, especially if your giveaway product is inexpensive. Unless a contest is fun, people won't be excited about it. And if they aren't excited about your contest, they won't feel the need to sign up.

- Promote your contest. You need to sell it well. Market your contest to get the word out so that people will come and check it out. Not everyone will be interested, but a few repins might make your contest visible to those who will be willing to take part. Get your audience excited about the product by providing information about it.

Engage with your Target Market

Connect with your followers just like you would respond to queries on forums, Instagram comments and Facebook posts. You can reply to comments on your pins, answer questions and respond to people's participation. If you do all that and respond to individuals directly, using their names, you are providing great customer service that your customers will definitely appreciate.

Consider commenting on your followers' pins. If you are active on followers' boards, they might be more inclined to reciprocate and repin some of your pins as well. Plus, your brand will get noticed.

Always interact and follow other popular boards. This will get you noticed among influential circles, and you can reap various benefits. Take a look at the pins such people follow and share, along with the kinds of boards they have. See how much they engage with their audience. Take inspiration and follow some of these other boards.

If you comment on the popular pins, your visibility will improve as a brand, not just because of the pinners themselves, but because of other users too. You will do better if you follow other well-known boards that are related to your business and industry than following random popular blogs, which will not benefit you in the slightest. You will also gain more by following boards in your own field.

Always try to understand what your followers are looking for and what interests them. In most cases, people will either come to you because you are answering a question they have, or because you can provide some insight into an interest of theirs. For a lot of industries, the Internet has become a saturated market. Trying to get started in such an atmosphere can be daunting. It's important to put in the work required to find gaps that need to be filled. You can concentrate on that area. A good example is the wedding market. Almost all areas are steeped in competition. However, mother-of-the-bride dresses still have some gaps that you can fill.

The richer content you can provide to your audience, the more likely they are to keep returning to you as a trusted source. Make sure you are adding to the knowledge that already exists elsewhere. If your content is exclusive, your audience might be more inclined to come back to your site rather than if it was a mere regurgitation of data that exists elsewhere. Ask yourself what will interest your audience.

Time is money. In today's world, which is based on instant gratification, especially online, timing is very important. You have to be conscious of what you can offer and be up-to-date on the latest advancements in the industry. There will be times when someone accidentally stumbles upon your website while looking for something, and you need to be aware of the driving catalysts as to how someone ends up on your site. If you know that, you will be able to more efficiently handle posts that drive traffic to your site.

Be reliable. Once you have your audience's attention, it is important not to lose it. Today's customer base is fickle. Unless you can be consistent and put out content in a timely fashion, your customers might drift to greener pastures. It is unlikely that a reader will remain loyal to you if you take an unexpected three-week hiatus. Everything is just a click away these days, and it won't be hard to lose followers if you don't pay attention to your schedules. If you stay consistent, your audience will view you as a reliable source and will keep returning to view your content.

Try to determine what time is most beneficial for you to post your content. People tend to be away from their computers on Fridays and Saturdays. So, putting out content on those days might get you fewer views than if you posted on a Thursday. Your audience will be eager for new material if you are able to post regularly.

Driving Traffic Back

The goal of this whole exercise, after all, is to drive traffic to your site. Rich Pins are a great tool to improve your chances of driving back traffic. They have extra content that makes them stand out from the grid of the layout of Pinterest. Integrating Rich Pins helps you a lot, and brands that use this feature have noticed an approximate 80 percent jump in their repin and pin ratio. Big brands like Wal-Mart and Target use Rich Pins to boost traffic, and there is no reason why this won't work for you.

There are different kinds of Rich Pins: movies, recipes, articles, places and products. These are all integrated with their own set of features that make them invaluable to each form of media. They will certainly direct traffic to your business, site or blog.

You can also create a board just for your blog posts, use as many of the article Rich Pins you have and organize them on their own board. If you put the board at the top of your page, it will be the first thing that your followers will see. This will help draw traffic to your site. It will also make it easier for your consumers to access since it is all in one easy-to-find board. People will definitely appreciate this.

Ensure link quality as this will be the path by which users will be led back to your site. Expired or deleted pages can be quite frustrating to users, and they might give up trying to visit your site if they find two or more dead links. Make sure you keep all your links updated. As mentioned before, give your customers navigating options on pages with out-of-stock products. Irrelevant links make it seem like you are spamming your followers' feeds.

Verifying your account will give you more authority and, therefore, more profile views. This will ultimately drive more traffic to your site. Don't forget to provide a good description of the content that you share and explain what your business is.

Optimize your content. Use SEO to your advantage and write compelling, targeted descriptions. If you are able to anticipate what users are looking for, you will be better situated to include these terms in your pin descriptions. However, remember to not sound like you're just filling the description with buzzwords.

Your description should encourage your readers to repin, share or visit your site for more information. If you inundate them with keywords, your audience might find it off-putting and this will negatively impact your ranking.

Board names should ideally contain one or two keywords that your pinners might use to search regularly. Use meaningful and relevant titles, and make them compelling. People will click on them if they interesting and fun or informative. Use SEO in your board description too, to make the most of Pinterest.

Using YouTube to Build Your Brand

Another great platform to promote your product is YouTube, the second most popular social media channel in the world after Google. If you are promoting your product online, YouTube has to be a part of it.

Different brands have different objectives for the online part of marketing. While some might be trying to promote their brand, others might be working toward generating brand awareness or driving sales. Physical products are not the only things that you can promote using this social channel; you can promote your services, your knowledge and even yourself. It helps you reach out to people so they hear you and see you.

Major advertisers and organizations often use YouTube to increase the awareness of their businesses or brands. Instead of pushing just products or services, YouTube pushes the brand with the help of videos, just the way traditional television advertising used to work. The reality is that videos are educational, entertaining and informational and create a deep impact on viewers. They can add a viral component to a brand. When someone posts a video on YouTube, that video sometimes creates a life of its own. It might be viewed by hundreds of thousands of viewers, posted on various blogs and websites, or be shared around different channels on the Internet. Just make sure you tweak the message you want to spread according to your target audience so that you can effectively generate traffic from the millions who use YouTube every day.

There are a variety of videos you can make depending on the type of product you are trying to sell in the marketplace. The key is to offer something that YouTube users want to see.

One way to achieve this is through YouTube's equivalent of an infomercial, which means a video that educates people on how to do something they are interested in or which functions as a teaser for another product that you want to sell. Here's an example. You are selling automobile parts. To market your product online, create a video on how to change the oil in your car or how to change the timing of an automobile's engine. Somewhere in the video, display your website address and/or your contact phone number. Upload this video to YouTube and if what you have created is rich in information, viewers will watch it; some of them might even click on the website to purchase your product.

The key is to provide useful information to users so that they want to watch the video. This will make your job of attracting those viewers to your website easier because they will want to get more information or even purchase your product. Notice that you haven't directly advertised the product here—you are directing the interested users to the site by means of information that might be of interest to them. This is called the Inform and Sell approach to promoting traffic.

Another approach you can take is creating a "How To" YouTube video. For example, back to our favorite example: say you are trying to sell a yoga mat. You can create a YouTube video showing your viewers how they can practice yoga to prevent certain types of ailments such as high blood pressure. The key is to offer useful information on how to do something. These types of videos have an element of practicality in them that draws audiences. Once you see people viewing your video, direct them to your website to sell your yoga mat. This is known as the Educate and Sell approach to selling your product as you are educating your users and then selling them your product.

Entertaining through a YouTube video can be another option you use to sell your product. This is likely to draw the attention of a large number of users as everyone likes to be entertained. What exactly "entertaining" is depends on what you are trying to sell. For example, if you are selling yoga mats, you can create a video around "Will it help you lose weight?" You can make this video extremely entertaining by showing different kinds of people practicing different exercises in different ways to meet their fitness goals— an overweight individual, an average weight male, a pregnant lady, etc. Then show how yoga can be an effective means to lose weight. This Entertain and Sell approach drives traffic to your website.

Advertising Options on YouTube

Before we look at the wonders of YouTube, here are some stats that speak for themselves:

- o In 2010, more than 13 million video hours were uploaded on YouTube and approximately 35 hours of video is uploaded every minute!

- o YouTube is available in more than 40 languages and 25 countries!

- o The demographic base of YouTube is between 18 and 45 years.

- o YouTube is the fourth largest website in the world of the Internet.

- o YouTube is the second largest video search engine, second only to Google.

The reason why YouTube is a promising platform for advertisers is that it has large traffic, huge search volumes, niche video channels and users from across the world who spend a great deal of time on the website.

If you are sold on the potential of YouTube and would like to consider the option of marketing on this platform, then you can choose from one of the following options:

Branded Video Channel

A branded video channel is like your home page on YouTube. You can create a branded channel to drive traffic toward your e-commerce website, engage with your consumers and also gain organic subscribers.

Anytime a user comes to the branded channel, their feature video will play automatically. Merchants can also feature other channels, videos, playlists, video blogs, etc. on their branded channel. You can get these channels for free or by paying a small premium. However, choosing the free plan will limit your branding options, whereas a premium plan gives you access to many in-built branding features.

YouTube Promoted Videos

By setting up a branded video channel, merchants can also run a YouTube promoted video campaign that is similar to the Google AdWords PPC (pay-per-click) advertising option.

Similar to the Sponsored Ads on Google, YouTube will also promote your videos that show up on the right-hand side of the page along with other relevant video search results. What makes it cost effective is that advertisers will only pay when the user clicks on the promoted ad.

You can create a promoted video campaign by:

- Choosing a relevant video.
- Creating an interesting promotional text.
- Mentioning the keywords that YouTube can use to trigger the promotion of your campaign.
- Setting a daily budget that you are willing to spend on your campaign.

You can use YouTube Insight to check the performance of your campaign. This free tool lets advertisers analyze detailed statistics like demographics, video hot spots, community engagement and sources of traffic.

YouTube In-Video Ads

Through the In-Video program, advertisers have the ability to select the videos in which they want their ads to appear. This way, they will be able to engage with the users who are watching the video. The ads can be displayed in text or image formats and are visible by overlaying the perimeter. The advertisers can pay on a CPC or CPM basis.

When your ad is clicked by the user, the video is paused and, depending upon the option the advertiser chose, the ad is displayed. The video resumes when the ad is closed. Advertisers can also use small banner ads to promote their product/service.

Google's Display Ad Builder can be used to create overlay or banner ads. This platform can be found on Google AdWords. The small businesses with no technical experience can also use the platform. The templates provided are easy to edit and understand and can be used to create banner ads for relevant YouTube videos.

Tips and Strategies

By now, you know that YouTube is a dominant and low-cost marketing channel that can unleash unlimited benefits for your brand. You can use YouTube videos or ads to reach a much larger audience than using conventional methods that have become ineffectual and expensive. Posting an ad on YouTube or making an interactive video is far more results-oriented than old-school methods of advertising.

Advertisers paid millions of dollars to buy a short 30-second spot for their ad during Super Bowl. With millions of views for this football playoff, it was easily one of the most heavily watched broadcasts in the history of US television, according to Nielsen Media Research.

Even better than Super Bowl ads, ads on YouTube are one of the best ways to get your product out there, targeting just the people you want to target, unlike TV that mass displays your ad and is only filtered to a select few, not to mention the exorbitant cost!

The best way to capitalize on YouTube ads is to include a link to your website or a landing page at the end of the video or the ad. The viewers who watch the ad following the video are more likely to convert as compared to those who come from other sources.

Here are some tips to use YouTube to promote your business:

Reach your Target Audience Consistently – Google is known to change its search algorithms constantly and can seriously impact your SEO efforts. PPC campaigns and Google AdWords can be expensive over time, and they may not always yield the results that you want to see. As such, using TrueView, Google's powerful video advertising platform, can bring your company into the spotlight. You receive a promotional spot that plays before the actual video and which can be skipped after five seconds. You can channel these ads to target your desired demographics and can even place your ad ahead of a competitor's video!

The two most important advantages of using TrueView are:

- It is 53 times likelier for the video ad to appear on top of Google search.
- Videos enjoy a 43 times greater click-through rate (CTR) than content without video.

Cost-Per-View Gives You Free Targeted Traffic – By using video ads on YouTube that are tracked and managed by AdWords, advertisers have the option to pay-per-view or pay-per-click. It is only when your viewer watches the ad for at least 30 seconds that you will be asked to pay. You will not have to pay for the ads that were never opened or were not viewed for the stipulated time. Imagine the almost-free exposure your brand can get through this!

The only trick here is to make a strong impression within the first four to five seconds. Your ad must make them click your link in this timeframe before they view your ad for 30 seconds.

Promote your Videos on Other Channels – Just uploading your videos to YouTube might not help. You should promote them on other channels by embedding them in your blog; emailing the link of your video to your contacts, friends and extended network; asking people to spread the word about your video; writing an article or blog about the video you have created and posting it in various forums and discussion boards; posting the video or sharing it on other social handles, such as Facebook, Twitter, etc. and asking others to retweet, share and repin in their networks too.

Chapter 7 – The Aftermath

Your product is launched, and you are doing whatever it takes to promote it—running various campaigns, promoting it on social handles, etc. You are getting sales and reviews too. Now it's time to look at the aftermath, which is as important as other steps in this entire selling process. So, let us look at some of the things you should be doing post-purchase.

Amazon Product Reviews – Positive or Negative

Amazon is a customer-centered platform. Your reviews on this platform transform sales into successes or disappointments at being kicked all the way back to the 20th page of product listings. When someone launches a product on Amazon, it is these reviews that tend to shorten the time lag between being "just another seller" to a "top-rated seller." Product reviews impact the conversion rate so much that they are a seller's powerful weapon to transform from "nobody" to "the world knows me." They impact the buying decisions of the shoppers and also act as good reference points for product improvement. Even marketers review them to understand the behavior and preferences of customers in the marketplace.

A seller should take several steps to stay competitive. He or she must provide

- A high-quality product
- fit-for-royalty customer service and

- an outstanding product page.

If you know these areas well, no one can stop you from becoming a popular seller on Amazon, assuming that you understand the basics around these three elements.

A weak point for every seller is negative reviews that buyers sometimes leave on their product page. Amazon never removes any negative feedback because it believes that reviews are meant to help buyers in making their purchase decisions and therefore shouldn't be tampered with. Being an Amazon seller, you must be mindful of any comments that your customer leaves for you, whether good or bad.

Although it is a tedious task, Amazon approves product review removals in two cases: Seller Feedback rating and Product reviews.

In the case of Customer Feedback, which includes concerns related to packaging, delivery, the condition of the product or product container and quality of customer service, FBA sellers can get negative feedback about damaged items or delayed delivery and these ratings hugely impact the overall profile of the seller and his business. In this case, you can absolutely get the negative rating removed as it is Amazon who is responsible for handling delivery, packing, shipping, etc. on your behalf.

If you receive a product review from a seller that has nothing to do with the product, it is definitely a removal candidate. Also, if Amazon finds the review to contain inappropriate content, promotional messages, offensive speech, hate content, promotion of unacceptable conduct or one-word reviews, it considers removing them from the product page. If an unhappy buyer posts multiple negative reviews for the same product (through multiple accounts), Amazon removes them.

Amazon encourages everyone to express their honest opinion for the benefit of other customers and sellers. Even if the opinion is in the form of a negative review, it is about his or her experience with the product, and these review comments are legit and acceptable on the platform. But if someone has formed a wrong opinion and is just trying to defame the seller, Amazon will look into the matter.

As a seller, if you feel you do not agree with the comment left by your buyer for any of the above-mentioned reasons, get in touch with Amazon. There are two ways to raise your concerns—you can report abuse and/or contact Amazon Seller support.

To know what type of reviews you are receiving, you must check them daily. After all, these customer reviews can have a huge impact on the success or failure of your business.

Reach Out to your Customers from Time to Time

Post-product launch strategies should include taking required actions to proactively communicate with your customers via post-sale emails from your Amazon dashboard. This builds a strong relationship with your customers and lets them know you care about their experience. A carefully drafted, thoughtful, purposeful email helps you build brand awareness, boost ratings, increase the response rate and converts potential customers into repeat buyers. A thoughtful strategy should include sending out three types of emails to each buyer post-purchase:

Thank You: This type of email builds brand awareness, which is otherwise a tedious task, particularly for third-party users. By writing a thank you note to your customers, they will know they have bought something from a unique brand, setting a foundation for future purchases and converting potential customers into repeat buyers. Thank you emails can do wonders for you and your brand.

Product Review Request: Amazon doesn't prompt buyers to leave a review for your product, so this is something you need to handle on your end. Encourage your buyers via a product review request email, asking them to share their experience of your product. This is an effective means of advertising for all potential customers who reach your product page.

Seller Feedback Request: Do not confuse Product Review with Seller Feedback as these are two different things. Seller feedback is the feedback your customer leaves for you, the seller. This feedback impacts the overall health of your account rating. These comments and ratings left by your customers can be treated as persuasive advertisements that can help build confidence in other potential customers, particularly those who are not familiar with you or your brand.

Apart from sending emails, you must respond to customer feedback within 24 hours, and that also includes holidays and weekends. Sellers should always promptly reply and cater to the needs of their customers as this builds confidence in them. If for some reason you are not able to check your messages frequently, you can create a separate account for this purpose and have someone else check it from time to time so customer queries are still responded to within 24 hours.

Check your Conversion Rate

Not just for Amazon, but for any type of business, the conversion rate is known to be one of the most investigated metrics to understand how a business is doing. First, understand that the conversion rate cannot be found under the title Conversion Rate in your seller account. Browse through the main menu and click on Reports. From the drop-down list, select Business Reports. Under the section Sales and Traffic, you will be able to see your daily business metrics which include the Order Item Session Percentage. This is the conversion rate. If you want to look at more meaningful data, look for the same column in the By ASIN report to get data for each item.

To understand how the conversion rate is derived, it is evaluated by dividing the Total Order Item (which is the total sales) by Sessions, which is the number of times customers visited your website/listing. This percentage is what gives you the conversion rate.

You know where to look for the conversion rate, and you also know how this conversion rate is calculated. Now it is important that you check and evaluate the rate on a regular basis as it helps you understand the success of your business. Although a specific definition doesn't exist to outline a good conversion rate or a bad conversion rate, the important points to keep in mind are that this rate is comparative and it should be considered along with the profit.

In the end, it's the sales and profit that a seller is interested in. If you have a superb conversion rate but are not meeting the daily profits, your business isn't going anywhere. Profits are definitely more important than the conversion rate. So, always look at improving the conversion rate in a way that it improves your overall profits.

Monitor Your Product Across Social Channels

You have launched your product, so now focus on the people and not on the product. The emphasis should be on how the launch affects you and your business and ensure you know what people are saying about it on different channels. You can even use various tools, such as Google Alerts to monitor this kind of information. Once you see the response from your customers, take time to return a comment, not just thanks or sorry, but going beyond that to provide a full customer experience. If possible, subscribe to comments so that you can keep a check on any future comments they might add. This way, it will be easy for you to go back to those comments and respond. This will go a long way toward helping people understand how important they are to you and will build trust and increase profits and sales.

Respond to positive reviews your customer has left for you to enhance your revenue generation. You can start by thanking your customer for his or her kind words. Proceed by sharing details of some of the other products you are selling. Certainly, you are promoting your business in the hope of getting more sales, and your customer will be happy to know there are other things to look at, if they are interested. Just add the Amazon link of any other product via the Insert a Product Link option. This will add your link as a hyperlink and will also help you increase traffic for this listing.

In case you have a negative comment, keep calm and respond soon. Keep an eagle eye on each and every review as, if you can respond when the buyer is online, you may be able to resolve the issue. However, this is not always possible, but you should always admit a mistake, correct any inaccuracies and offer a resolution to the problem.

Monitor Your Inventory From Time to Time

Inventory management is important at each stage of your product selling business. It is essential throughout the year as the momentum might increase as you run various campaigns and marketing strategies. With time, you will see an increase in click rates, conversions and sales. If you do not have enough inventory to match the needs of your customers, the momentum is eventually lost, and this leads to a reduction in click rates, conversion rates and all that you have invested in advertising your brand. To sustain your place in the marketplace, it is important that you continuously monitor your inventory levels and see to it that there is no gap in your ability to meet the demands of your customers. Monitoring the inventory is particularly important right after you run a campaign and also during the holiday season as this is when more sales happen. If you fail to meet the expectations of your customers due to mismanaged inventory, you could lose out on some of the biggest opportunities of the year.

One of the common mistakes made by sellers and vendors in inventory management is not keeping a check on the velocity of sales of their products. Why is this important? Keeping a tab on the sales rate helps you understand how much inventory you have left, so you'll know whether this is sufficient to cater to the needs of your customers in the days to come. If you are an FBA seller on Amazon, you should always take into consideration the time it takes to manufacture the product and reach Amazon. Failure to replenish the products within the time left for the inventory to get to zero leads to disasters.

The seller needs to decide the momentum of sales in order to avoid running into stock-outs. In the event that stock-out happens, some brands choose to switch to Fulfillment By Merchant (FBM) from FBA. But this can work only if you keep a constant check on your inventory levels so that you can switch to FBM to keep a steady stock of your product.

In the event that you run out of your FBA inventory, you have the option where the seller fulfills the delivery to the customers. Although it is a good option to avoid a stock-out situation, as a consistent model, it has its own issues. To be able to offer the same experience as FBA to your customers, you need to replicate that service which includes free returns, free shipping, delivery services and so on. In general, FBM is not recommended as a core business approach. Being a brand owner, you won't receive the benefits as being an FBA seller. In the FBM model, one can see a huge dip in conversion rates and sales as people tend to filter out the products that do not adhere to FBA standards. FBA has led to a psychological transformation of the shoppers when it comes to buying products online, and they have become so used to free returns, free shipping and fast deliveries that they do not want anything that is not close to FBA standards.

The inventory also impacts your campaigns. If you run into a stock-out condition, all the effort and time you have invested in building the productivity of your PPC or some other campaign will have been in vain. The ranking of your product will be drastically impacted, and even when the inventory is returned, it will take time to rebuild the momentum you have now lost.

So you can see that inventory management is an important task that should be done regularly. Here are some ways you can improve the inventory management process and organize your inventory effectively:

Use inventory management software – As an FBA seller, you can use any tools that are available to manage inventories that integrate with Amazon. These tools not only help you track your inventory but also provide real-time analytics about sales and conversion, which are important to give your brand a competitive edge. This way you will be able to better analyze the demand for your product and provide better service to your customers through tracking information.

Monitor supplies regularly – If your suppliers are not delivering your product on time, it can greatly impact your ability to manage the inventory. Therefore, there is a need to monitor your inventory closely on a regular basis to avoid delays in deliveries. Some of the key pointers you should watch for are:

- receipt dates
- agreed delivery dates
- quantity ordered
- quantity received and
- condition of the delivered package.

However, monitoring all this isn't an issue if you are an FBA seller as FBA automates the entire fulfillment process.

Fundamentals of Bookkeeping

According to studies, one of the biggest challenges Amazon sellers face today is bookkeeping and accounting. Most sellers on Amazon love to talk about optimized listings, product niches, etc., but when you turn the conversation to taxes, balance sheets and asset management, they shudder. This is because most sellers spend their time and focus on generating more sales, driving traffic to their listings, finding experienced private labelers, setting up optimized listings on Amazon, getting reviews and running campaigns, identifying demands, etc. But when it comes to assessing and managing the financial part of their business, they feel uncomfortable.

So, let's look at the basics of accounting and bookkeeping practices so that you can tackle the financial part of your business wisely.

There are two key financial reports that every seller on Amazon must be familiar with: the Profit and Loss Statement and the Balance Sheet. These tools will help you get to the heart of your business, which is financial statistics, and retrieve data that is essential to make key business decisions. Without these reports, you will not have a complete picture of how your business is doing.

Profit and Loss Statement

The Profit and Loss Statement is a tool to evaluate performance, and in large businesses, it is the primary and most important document used to show the capabilities of the organization. It gives the overall picture of what the net income, which is evaluated by adding all the expenses—your monthly Amazon Inventory Storage fees, expenditure on various campaigns and other marketing activities, shipping, etc. and then subtracting this amount from the total revenue. It is this net income that is needed to determine how much your taxable income is for the year.

If you are a seller on Amazon, this Profit and Loss Statement will come in handy when you want to evaluate your past performance. How did you perform last year? How was it compared to the previous year? While setting up this statement, you must remember to consider the type of accounting method you are planning to use; it can be either

- **Cash Basis** – the revenue is reported in the Profit and Loss Statement for the period the customer pays the cash.
- **Accrual Basis** – the revenue is reported in the statement when the business is owed money before the customer pays the cash.

The Balance Sheet

The Balance Sheet is used to evaluate the overall health of your business. The two statements go hand-in-hand. Only when you have the details of both statements, will you be able to analyze how your business is actually performing. The Profit and Loss Statement doesn't show all the components of the business; it doesn't take into consideration the amount you borrowed for your next order, the value of unsold inventory, sales tax you owe, etc. All this is covered in the Balance Sheet, which makes it unique as it is the only document that displays an accurate snapshot of the financial health of your business.

The Accounting Equation is a method that helps you understand the financial shape of your company and the way different components of a Balance Sheet are linked to each other. Based on the business structure, the equation varies from company to company. For instance, if you are the sole owner of your company and the Amazon seller, the structure of your business will be considered a sole proprietorship. In this case, the Accounting Equation would be:

Assets = Owner's Equity + Liabilities

Where:

- Assets refer to your resources.
- Liabilities are what you owe to other individuals.
- Owner's equity is the difference between the two—assets minus liabilities.

A Balance Sheet is a two-sided document that lists assets on one side and liabilities and owner's equity on the other. As the name suggests, the aim is to balance both sides of this sheet, which means the total of both sides should be the same, confirming that the Balance Sheet of your organization is balanced.

Although the Profit and Loss Statement and Balance Sheet are two key documents for any business, there are a few other statements that are also taken into consideration:

Cash Flow Statement

A cash flow statement helps sellers understand the flow of capital that goes into and out of a business for a specific accounting period. This statement is unique because no other report captures the cash flow for a specific time frame. FBA sellers generally use this report quarterly.

Taking the starting cash balance, which is the company's total cash balance obtained from the Balance Sheet, all that flows into the system is treated as positive events and the outflows are negative. For the cash flow, the inflows and outflows are considered for three activities:

- **Operations** – These are the primary sources as well as the consumers of your business' cash. They include your sales income, income tax payment and the cost you pay to suppliers and freight forwarders.
- **Investment activities** – These are the selling and buying of assets which are not linked to the inventory.
- **Finance activities** – These include activities, such as borrowing money, taking a loan to pay for the inventory, repaying the amount borrowed, etc.

Now you should understand the important financial statements that you should be using to understand the financial health of your business as an Amazon seller.

Taxes for Amazon Sellers

Sales Tax

Taxes have always been a gray area for beginners as most don't seem to have a clear picture of how they works. Let us describe a clear step-by-step process of sales tax collection through your Seller Account on Amazon. Once you understand the basics, you will be able to determine how to apply for sales tax, how to set up your account to automatically collect the tax and how to automate the process.

Certainly, Amazon has given all of us a new way of looking at things—our shopping experience, buying things online, etc. It has also changed the way we used to think about taxes; Amazon has taken various steps to shield its FBA users from the long arm of revenue officers. With its increasing curve and need to have more investments in the organization, it has opened various warehouses. Opening these warehouses has required Amazon to state criteria for the responsibility and legal terms required to collect, file and remit sales tax. This criterion is known as nexus. It is the presence of a business within a state and something you would consider while looking at requirements to manage sales tax. This presence can be in any form—an employee, a workplace or a warehouse. Here are some examples of sales tax nexus:

- **Employee nexus**: You live in Texas and operate out of Texas, but you have your sister helping you from Florida. As you are operating out of Texas and your sister is in Florida, you have sales tax nexus in Texas as well as Florida, and you need to collect sales tax from your buyers in these two states.
- **Home state nexus**: You live in Florida and operate out of Florida. Because you are physically present in Florida, you have sales tax nexus in Florida, and that's why you need to collect sales tax from your buyers in this state.

If you have the sales tax nexus in the state you are operating in, and if you are operating from any of the 45 US states, you are required to charge sales tax to your customers. This tax is applicable to all customers no matter what they purchase. It is a pass-through tax that you as the seller will hold before remitting it to the legal authorities. These taxes are used to fund various state initiatives and projects including funding schools, building roads, etc. However, the sales tax rules and laws for all 45 states in the US are different. These even vary by locality and state.

Consider an example: State A requires you to renew your sales tax permit, but state B doesn't. Therefore, you must get in touch with your state's tax department or consult an expert in this domain before you even start your business.

Once you have determined the nexus you have in a state, you must register with that state's registration department by visiting their website to know how to collect the appropriate sales tax. Complete the registration process so that your business will have a permit to collect sales tax at a rate determined by the tax authority.

Income Tax

The IRS needs to know your annual income from your Amazon business, which means not just the cost of products but everything. You must take into considerations deductions like Amazon fees, Amazon shipping charges, FBA subscription fees, FBA inventory charges, health insurance plans, etc.

Chapter 8 – Business Structures for your FBA Business

When someone decides to start a business, one of the key decisions to make is what the structure of the business should be. Selecting the type of business structure can sometimes be really overwhelming, so it is good to know the pros and cons, tax structures, features, etc. that each of the structures can contribute.

The most common forms of business are:

Sole Proprietorships: The easiest business structure to create is a sole proprietorship. The business is owned by one person who is the sole proprietor. In this type of business structure, there is no difference between the business and the owner in legal terms; it is meant for those who do business without any partners, associates or state and federal regulations. Some examples of sole proprietors could be freelance photographers, writers, graphic designers, etc.; essentially, those who work independently with few legal liabilities.

If you choose to run and manage the business as a sole proprietor, any responsibility of the business is your personal responsibility. This is because you are solely responsible for the business and all its activities—legally as well as financially. In other words, the debts incurred by the business are your personal debts, and any dispute related to the business is your issue. On the other side, you are not answerable to anyone; you are your boss, you are your business.

Pros of a Sole Proprietorship:

- Being the business owner, you are solely responsible for all the business decisions, and there are no federal or state regulations in regards to the organizational structure.
- A sole proprietorship structure is comparatively easy to form and is inexpensive. While it doesn't require you to complete any legal paperwork or filing of any other necessary documents, you must register your business within the filing agency of your state or province.
- There are no business taxes involved in this form of business. Since the business is not taxed separately, all the profits are filed on the personal income tax return of the sole proprietor of the business. The owner is free to either take the profits or reinvest for the growth of the business. The tax rates are the lowest for this type of business structure.

Cons of a Sole Proprietorship:

- There are limited financial options available for a sole proprietorship. An investor cannot offer additional funding as it is the responsibility of sole proprietor to fund his business through his own savings or loans. Even the availability of loans is an issue. Banks and lenders are hesitant to invest in such a business or to offer a loan because being a sole owner makes it difficult to have a consistent cash flow.

- There are no lawsuits to protect the rights of a sole proprietor. As well as being solely responsible for the business, they are solely responsible for all damages incurred. In the event that the business is sued, the customer has the right to sue not just for the business assets but the personal assets of the sole proprietor as well.

Partnerships: This is a business structure where two or more individuals operate a business as co-owners. Each individual contributes property, capital, labor and expects to share in both profits and losses of the company. This type of business structure requires the individuals to file annual data regarding their gains, losses, income, etc. but there is no need to pay the income tax. All the profits and losses are passed to the partners.

Although on legal grounds there is no requirement to draft a partnership agreement, it is always advisable to have a written agreement to avoid any kind of dispute. But if there is no partnership agreement and a dispute arises, state partnership law that applies, which is the generic regulation that is applicable to all sorts of partnerships. According to this, profits and losses should be equally divided between partners. However, in certain states, it depends on the contribution made by each partner. As this is an umbrella type of rule, you should draft a partnership agreement that lists topics that are key to the business, such as splitting of profits and losses, etc.

Pros of a Partnership:

- A partnership is a very simple and straightforward business structure as there is no formal paperwork needed to form this structure. However, it is good to have a written agreement to avoid disputes.
- A partnership allows individuals to share their skills as well as capital to start a business. As businesses are often expensive ventures, it helps when more than one person can help financially to create the company. It even mitigates the risk factor.
- A partnership brings together talents and allows individuals to brainstorm ideas.

Cons of a Partnership:

- Partnerships collapse easily.
- Partners are required to pay personal income tax on the net profits from the business.
- All partners involved in the partnership are liable for debts and other liabilities.

Limited Liability Company (LLC): An LLC is a kind of business structure that combines elements of partnerships and corporations while eradicating some of the undesirable elements of each. It is a comparatively new business type that has become quite popular worldwide. An LLC is allowed by state statute, and as each state has its own set of rules and regulations, one must check these specifications before starting an LLC. The owners of this kind of business are known as members, and as most states do not have any restrictions when it comes to types of owners; members can be corporations, individuals, etc.

LLCs can be single-member or multiple-member. Each member has their own unit of ownership which shows the percentage of business they own and the amount of influence they have on vital business matters. All the owners own the complete business and its assets, plus they have a say in the decisions. The members are liable to pay taxes on the business profits but only on their personal returns, while their personal assets and accounts are not liable for any legalities or business debts.

Pros of LLCs:

- LLCs offer their members protection against personal liabilities. If any creditor files a lawsuit against the company, it does not affect the members personally. The personal assets of the members are always secured no matter what happens in the business.
- LLCs offer the business liability protection.
- There are no restrictions on ownership as there can be any number of owners. These owners can be individuals, corporations or even other entities.
- LLCs offer flexibility in terms of tax status as you can choose your own way to be taxed based on what you feel is best for your business. You can even be taxed as a corporation as your business structure follows an LLC approach.
- There is no need to file tax returns separately as with standard taxation; the profits and losses of

the business can be reported on the personal tax returns.

Cons of LLCs:

- As the LLC structure is very flexible, investors might hesitate to invest in the business.
- An LLC structure has pass-through taxes. Although this is seen as a positive, it might be worrisome for shareholders when they do not receive their dividends.
- Lack of authority can lead to disputes and issues.

Corporations: Just like the LLC, corporations are created and managed by state law. But what differentiates corporations from other business structures is that it exists as a legal entity as per federal and state law. It is a legal tax structure and separate from the owners or individuals who control or run it. This means the entity is liable to have debts, make contracts, pay taxes and sustain a life of its own, separate from its owners or managers. There are two types of corporations:

S Corporations – pass corporate credits, income and deductions through shareholders for the purposes of federal tax; they have a special tax status with the IRS. These corporations detail the flow-through of their losses as well as income on their personal tax returns. They are evaluated at their specific income tax rates, and this means prevention of double taxation on company income. They are even liable to pay taxes at a certain level for passive income.

C Corporations – are legal business structures that can choose to structure themselves to limit the financial and legal liabilities of their owners. They are an alternative to the S corporation structure where:

- profits are passed through to owners and taxed at the individual level.
- legal protection is provided due to limited liability but is taxed similarly to sole proprietors.

So, there is double taxation. When this type of a company generates revenue, it files its tax return on this income. The income, after deducting the salaries and business expenses, is liable to tax. The net income is also distributed among the shareholders (as dividends). The dividends are the income of the shareholders and are reported on an individual tax return. Hence, the profit from these types of companies is taxed at an individual tax rate as well as at a corporation tax rate.

Although this double taxation is seen as a negative point, it gives the business the ability to reinvest profits in the growth of the company.

The Differences Between S Corporations and C Corporations

Taxation: One of the key differences to be considered when evaluating the two types of corporations is taxation. While C corporations are separate entities that file a corporate tax return and pay at a corporate level, S corporations are just pass-through entities and therefore, taxes are not filed at the corporate level. There is a possibility of double taxation in C corporations because the income is distributed among shareholders in the form of dividends (which is treated as shareholders' personal income). The tax is then paid on this income first at the corporate level and then on dividends at the personal level. However, in S corporations, as the profits/losses are just passed through the business, any tax due is paid by the owners at the personal level. The personal income tax in both C corporations and S corporations is payable on the total income whether it is in the form of dividends or the salary drawn from the corporation.

Ownership: Regarding ownership, there are no restrictions for C corporations, but there are for S corporations:

- S corporations cannot have more than 100 shareholders, and these shareholders must be US residents or citizens.
- S corporations cannot have C corporations, LLCs, partnerships or other S corporations as the owners; they may be certain estates, trusts or individuals.
- S corporations have only a single class of stocks.

Conclusion

Thank you for reading this book.

I hope you found this book to be useful. If it did help you, would you be kind enough to leave a positive review on Amazon?

Good luck on your journey and all the best!

Bonus Chapter – Beginner's Guide to Merch By Amazon

You know everything about Amazon FBA, so now let me give you something extra – another great business option: Merch By Amazon. This is a T-shirt printing service provided by Amazon that lets you create and sell T-shirt designs on demand. You can create and list the designs on Amazon for free! This way you do not have to ship the T-shirts to fulfillment centers using their FBA service and wait to see if people will buy them. This is the beauty of Merch By Amazon. You list your T-shirt, and get paid per piece. All you need to do is list the design by uploading the picture, setting a price and other key specifications and let the platform do the magic for you.

The only limitation to Merch is that it only allows you to sell T-shirts now. But don't worry, as Amazon has plans to branch out to other forms of merchandise if this works out well.

Steps to Create Designs on Merch by Amazon

1. Create Your Account

As Merch By Amazon is quite popular among sellers and buyers, the only way Amazon could think of managing this flood was by letting members sign up based on their position on a waiting list. The waiting time can be anything from three weeks to three months. So, yes, you need to have patience—lots of it!

Once the wait is over and your invitation to join the platform is approved, you can sign up and log into your account. Amazon will then ask you for basic information before you can get started listing the T-shirts.

2. Think of your Game Strategy

Like any other business, you need to have a strong business strategy before you get started. So, before you upload the design, have the action plan ready by analyzing: your target audience, ideas for the T-shirt designs, how to get the images, what the trending designs will be, whether you will able to Photoshop the images, etc.

Once you analyze various things and come up with a game plan, you will see that you can create 25 designs on Amazon to start with. Amazon has various Merch tiers, and each tier comes with its own settings and limitations. For instance, when you are Tier 1, you can create 25 designs. When you are Tier 2, you can create 100 designs and so on. Having different levels like this rewards those who are capable of selling designs by upgrading those sellers to the next tier. At the same time, it doesn't help a new seller who hardly knows the business.

3. Understand the Listing

Before you start uploading, understand how the listing looks and what all is required to list a design on Amazon. The best way to understand this is to click any existing listing and check various attributes. For example, you can view the ranking of a T-shirt to see how well the product is doing in the marketplace.

Go to any Merch T-shirt and click on its listing. Now scroll to the description section of the product and check its Amazon Best Sellers Rank. If an item doesn't have any associated rank, it means none of the T-shirts have been sold. Generally, people choose to go with products that have a BSR of less than 100,000 because you can use these designs as your inspiration to see what it is that customers like. While you must not copy the design, you can get inspiration and add your own creativity.

Apart from the ranking, you will see that all the listings have two common attributes—the sizing chart and a white tag. The sizing chart compares the dimension of the T-shirt in various standards, while the white tag will have brand details.

4. Analyze the Competition

Knowing your competitors is key in the marketplace. Just checking the rank of a product is not sufficient; you must also think about the competition—will this be a good option to target my audience? I would suggest that you pick a T-shirt design that is competitive but has sellers with a low ranking. This means the T-shirt design is being liked by people, but if the sellers have a low ranking, there is a chance to fight and win the competition in the market.

5. Create the Merch T-shirt Design

Along with the log-in details, Amazon provides you certain templates that you can see in the templates tab of your dashboard. When you open one of these templates, you will see the instructions written to how to create the design. The instructions are pretty clear and easy to follow. All you need to know is how to use Photoshop. If not Photoshop, it can be GIMP or Pixlr.

Once you have the software ready, start editing the template. You can add quotes, vectors and anything that you would like into your T-shirt design. One thing to remember is that if you are using vectors (defined in the following section), you need good quality images or else the artwork might look pixelated. Once the design is complete, you can save it as a PNG file or upload it to Amazon. You can also save a copy as a PSD (editable file) so that you can edit and make changes to it later.

Now, other than the basic tool to edit the template, there are various other research tools available to help you with various things, for example, MerchResearch, Vector Me, FreePic, etc.

Research: MerchResearch helps you search any phrase you enter in the Merch category within Amazon. This saves the time you spend in going back and forth.

Copyrights: While designing your Merch, do not infringe upon any copyrights; know that all designs must pass the approval process. This is because if you use someone else's work or copywritten image or content, you might run into huge risks. Amazon can even shut down your complete account without giving you time to explain. If you are not sure about copyright terms or if the material you are planning to use belongs to someone, use tools that help you to clearly determine ownership.

Vectors: These are images that help enhance a design without losing the quality of the image. For example, if you have a bird quote, you can probably find a bird vector that can add beauty to your design. These vectors add creativity to the design and give you ideas. Use tools or websites that help you find vectors.

Mistakes to Avoid While Using Merch by Amazon

Let us look at some of the things you must not do to keep your account safe while using Merch By Amazon (MBA).

1. Using keywords that are not related to your listing.

When researching the keywords for your listing on Amazon, you might find that people include unrelated keywords as well as phrases in their listings. They might be doing that to get more traffic, but using unrelated keywords or phrases is completely against the terms and conditions of Amazon, and something you must avoid if you want to keep your Amazon account safe. This is one of the reasons Amazon restricts the description to certain characters so that they can fight spamming. Amazon is taking additional steps to continue to combat this problem.

Never listen to people who suggest fluffing your title or description with keywords that are not related to your listing. You might be fine today, but with the new terms

Amazon is developing, you could see a banned account one day.

2. Using parody and satire

While you might be able to do something really amazing by adding parody to your listing in the right niche, it doesn't have to be included your MBA designs. Stay away from satirical designs when you are dealing with Amazon, as they can take down the design the moment they find it.

3. Adding fake reviews

This is one of the most important things to keep in mind. You must stay away from fake reviews and keep two things in mind: never even think about leaving a fake review on your competition listing and never purchase/request that someone write fake reviews on your listing. While researching some products, you might have noticed that some reviews do not have a verified tag underneath them—this is an indication that the review might not be an authentic one.

What some sellers have started doing is looking at a listing of their competitive sellers and leaving a fake bad review on their listing. Although this review will not have a verified tag, the customers might just see the one-star rating without noticing the missing verified tag. So, you can save yourself by getting in touch with the MBA customer team and getting such fake reviews removed.

Never ask someone to leave you a five-star fake review on your listing. This is not just against the terms and conditions of Amazon; you can even be sued for this. Be fair at all times!

CPSIA information can be obtained
at www.ICGtesting.com
Printed in the USA
LVHW011332080920
665327LV00004B/739